D0858103

CZECH THEATRE DESIGN IN THE TWENTIETH CENTURY

STUDIES IN

THEATRE HISTORY & CULTURE

Edited by Thomas Postlewait

Edited by Joe Brandesky

Czech Theatre Design
IN THE TWENTIETH CENTURY

METAPHOR & IRONY REVISITED

UNIVERSITY OF IOWA PRESS   IOWA CITY

University of Iowa Press, Iowa City 52242
Copyright © 2007 by the University of Iowa Press
www.uiowapress.org
All rights reserved
Printed in the United States of America
Design by Richard Hendel

The University of Iowa Press is a member of Green Press Initiative
and is committed to preserving natural resources.

Printed on acid-free paper

ISBN-10: 1-58729-525-3
ISBN-13: 978-1-58729-525-6
LCCN: 2006936552

07 08 09 10 11 C 5 4 3 2 1

PN 2091
.S8
C94
2007

0123977366

CONTENTS

PREFACE

The transitory nature of theatre has long been recognized by historians as a central problem to its study. How is it possible to understand a given production in a given time without visual referents? To be sure, collections have been amassed and volumes written that attempt to provide enough evidence for the mind's eye to capture the ephemeral activities of theatres past. It has become my scholarly mission to display the visual residua of Czech production activities through public exhibitions, to open the archives to audiences removed from the sources. Since it is my view that the richness of Czech theatre can be fully understood only through the comparison of written descriptions and visual referents, this book is comprised of the contents—catalogs and images—of two exhibitions shown in the United States between 2000 and 2005: Metaphor and Irony: Czech Scenic and Costume Design 1920–1999 and Metaphor and Irony 2: František Tröster and Contemporary Czech Theatre Design.

The disparity between textual and visual analyses of theatre productions first became clear to me during my studies at the University of Kansas. As a student of Russian and Soviet theatre under the tutelage of William Kuhlke, I became familiar with traditional text-based research and writing. We utilized all the images available at the time, but the Cold War limited our ability to see what had been done. Instead, a few grainy black-and-white images were recycled from publication to publication. Two experiences with guest artists from the Eastern Bloc in 1987 altered my limited perspectives. The first was the opportunity to work with Soviet writer-in-residence Edvard Radzinsky. I directed a translation of his play Lunin, and acted as his guide during his visit to the University of Kansas. Almost at the same time, the Czech designer Jaroslav Malina, whose work is represented in this book, made his first visit to our campus. Malina exhibited some of his designs in the corridor of Murphy Hall at the University of Kansas and I passed them daily on my way to rehearsals. The convergence of my conversations with Radzinsky and my initiation to Czech action design through Malina's exhibition invigorated my conceptions of their respective theatre cultures.

A few years later, after I joined the theatre faculty of Ohio State University at Lima, I visited Prague, Moscow, and Leningrad with a group sponsored by the Association for Theatre in Higher Education. During this 1991 trip I was reacquainted with Jaroslav Malina in Prague. The 1989 Velvet Revolution had created opportunities for scholars and artists to travel freely. Malina soon became a frequent visitor to Ohio and I had firsthand experience with Czech theatre practices. But it was in Leningrad, at the Museum for Theatre and Music, that the first opportunity to mount a theatre exhibition revealed itself. Our group viewed numerous designs by the artists of the Ballets Russes—Léon Bakst, Aleksandr Benois, Aleksandr Golovin—and a painter-designer named Boris Anisfeld. Our Russian hosts asked us if we had information about Anisfeld, because they knew very little about his career after his emigration to the United States in 1918. They knew Anisfeld designed the world premiere for Sergei Prokofiev's opera *Love for Three Oranges* (Chicago, 1921) but had never seen examples of his work for this production. At the Lawrence and Lee Theatre Research Institute at Ohio State University, I had recently seen designs that Anisfeld completed for Metropolitan Opera productions. Through the intercession of valuable and knowledgeable Russian and American colleagues and financial support from my campus, the first Boris Anisfeld and the Theatre exhibit of designs and paintings opened in Saint Petersburg, Russia, in October 1994. There followed two more Russian theatre design exhibits before I determined to undertake what became known as the Czech Metaphor and Irony exhibits. A few words about the development of these exhibits help to explain the path to this book.

During the late nineties I developed an exhibit called Spectacular Saint Petersburg: One Hundred Years of Russian Theatre Design with the Saint Petersburg State Museum for Theatre and Music and the Columbus Museum of Art. I simultaneously worked with designers and scholars in Prague, including Helena Albertová, on an exhibition project that would feature the Czech design legacy. Albertová served as vice-director of the Theatre Institute in Prague and was the commissioner general of the 1995 Prague Quadrennial (PQ). She was also a frequent visitor to nearby Miami University, which provided me the opportunity to meet her and develop the exhibit. After meetings in Prague with Albertová and Ondřej Černy, director of the Theatre Institute, Helena and I agreed to produce an exhibit of Czech theatre design. As co-curators, we determined that the Czech exhibit would be historical in scope and would include deceased designers from the early part of the century as well as those who were currently working. We also decided to include a few designs shown as part of the Czech national exhibit at the 1999 Prague Quadrennial. The organizing sponsor for the exhibit in the United States was the Ohio Arts Council. Its director, Wayne Lawson, visited Prague during PQ and selected several items for inclusion in the exhibit. That year, the Czech national exhibit was awarded the Golden Triga, the main prize of the Prague Quadrennial. As the time for display of our exhibition in the United States drew closer, a title emerged: Metaphor and Irony.

Through the roughly eighty-year span it covered, the exhibit Metaphor and Irony: Czech Scenic and Costume Design 1920–1999 traced the influences of European art movements and philosophies on theatre artists in the Czech homeland, that is, Bohemia and Moravia. Although the selection process was difficult, we were pleased to include eighty items in the exhibit that were shown at four venues between 2000 and 2001: the Riffe Gallery, Columbus, Ohio; the Civic Center Gallery, Lima, Ohio; the Tobin Gallery, Marion Koogler McNay Museum of Art, San Antonio, Texas; and the Spencer Museum of Art, Lawrence, Kansas. The Ohio State University Lawrence and Lee Theatre Research Institute subsequently acquired a number of the items shown in this exhibit as additions to its Czech design collection. The first Metaphor and Irony exhibit was specifically developed to provide an overview of twentieth-century theatre design in the Czech Republic. It described and incorporated modernist trends and the adjustments necessitated by a range of political changes in this Central European country over the course of that century.

After the success of the first project, I decided to pursue another Czech exhibit that would focus on currently active designers. Once again I worked with co-curator Helena Albertová, and we used a calendar similar to the one for the first Metaphor and Irony exhibit. We would select final items for the exhibit from the Czech national exhibit at the 2003 Prague Quadrennial. However, our focus on this process and on contemporary artists was interrupted while Albertová was working with the architect for PQ, Martin Tröster, son of František Tröster, arguably the most influential of the mid-twentieth-century Czech designers. Many of Tröster's best designs had been confiscated and made part of national collections during the prior regime. This fact contributed to the omission of Tröster's work in the first Metaphor and Irony exhibit. Martin Tröster revealed that a number of his father's designs were still in storage: Helena asked for and was given access to these designs and we agreed that a selection of the works should be included in the exhibit.

We now addressed the question of uniting Tröster's historically important designs with our announced theme of contemporary Czech design. Fortunately, the solution was simple and self-evident since the connections between Tröster's work and that of Czech contemporary designers were multiple and varied. Several designers from the sixties and seventies had been his students. Some of them eventually taught the next generations of designers, and still others gained their education indirectly, from their exposure to the work of those who had been in Tröster's circle. This "inherited" tradition had an influence on those who carried it forward as well as those who preferred to find new ways, cutting ties with the past. In one way or another, the works of all the contemporary Czech designers included in this exhibit had a relationship with the work of František Tröster. My Czech colleagues liked the title of the first exhibit, so the second became Metaphor and Irony 2: František Tröster and Contemporary Czech Theatre Design.

After initial inquiries, it was clear that several venues wanted the exhibit, but none wanted to serve as its organizing entity. My campus administration agreed to allow me to organize the exhibit through Ohio State University at Lima. The advantages of serving as organizer for the exhibit were many: more items were exhibited (over a hundred frames with more than three hundred individual items); a larger catalog was produced (printed in Prague with a hundred illustrations); and additions to the exhibit schedule could be expedited (a third of the Czech items were requested in April 2005 for an exhibit at the World Bank in July 2005). Among the items exhibited were costumes, puppets, models, and framed designs. The space required to stage a show of this size led some exhibitors to split the items among several nearby locations. All told, Metaphor and Irony 2 was seen at six venues between 2004 and 2005: Bowling Green State University's Fine Arts Center Gallery, Bowling Green, Ohio; the University of Toledo's Studio Theatre Gallery, Toledo, Ohio; Ohio State University's Hopkins Hall Gallery, Jerome Lawrence and Robert E. Lee Theatre Research Institute, Gladys Keller Snowden Gallery, Columbus, Ohio; the Marion Koogler McNay Art Museum's Tobin Gallery, and the University of the Incarnate Word's

Semmes Gallery, San Antonio, Texas; the World Bank, Washington, D.C.; and Ohio State University at Lima's Martha W. Farmer Theatre for the Performing Arts Gallery.

The catalog for Metaphor and Irony 2, written in English, was produced and printed in Prague. I served as editor for the project, a process made possible because the document was produced digitally. Once the exhibition was over, the images scanned for the catalog remained. I then decided to make the visual materials from the exhibits available in a combined book-CD form. But I wanted this project to be more effective than past efforts.

In 1999 I organized and edited a CD-ROM to accompany the exhibition entitled Spectacular Saint Petersburg: One Hundred Years of Russian Theatre Design. The director of the Columbus Museum of Art, Irvin Lippman, decided to forgo the typical printed catalog and instead build a comprehensive CD-ROM to capture all the images from the exhibition. I worked with several individuals: we designed the features, researched the materials, acquired the rights to reproduce images, and edited text for the disk. The executed disk had an interactive timeline, biographies, scenarios, and music. However, the platform used for the CD-ROM quickly became outdated, thus limiting its effectiveness after only a short period of time. After working on the edits for the Metaphor and Irony 2 catalog I felt that the technology had developed sufficiently to make an effective Czech theatre design book project with accompanying CD. This time readers can open the images and documents on the disk using their computer browser, extending the usefulness of the CD.

The result is this book, which is meant to provide supplementary essays and images for readers of Jarka Burian's books, *Leading Creators of Twentieth-Century Czech Theatre* (Routledge, 2002) and *Modern Czech Theatre: Reflector and Conscience of a Nation* (University of Iowa Press, 2000). Burian studied the Czech actors, directors, and designers in the context of the history and culture of the tumultuous century they inhabited. *Czech Theatre Design in the Twentieth Century: Metaphor and Irony Revisited* focuses on examples of the designers' works, their lives in the form of biographies, and critics' views of the place of Czech theatre design in the world. Along with my essay and those by Věra Ptáčková, Dennis P. Christilles, Delbert Unruh, and Marie Zdeňková that were previously published in the Metaphor and Irony catalogs and have been reedited and updated, it contains a limited number of black-and-white images along with reference numbers for the color images on the disk.

For example, in the book a reference to TROS01 will be consistent with the first viewable image for František Tröster on the CD. The complete list of images and their reference numbers and production information is available in an appendix to the text. The essays and biographies in this book can also be found on the CD with clickable links to the images and biographies. Additionally, several *in situ* photographs of exhibited designs not included in the original catalogs have been added to the CD. The works of the designers included here supply an integral, valuable, and heretofore largely unseen facet of the Czech contributions and their relationship to developments in the world of modern theatre. These visual referents provide ample evidence of the quality and variety of Czech scenic and costume design in the twentieth century.

ACKNOWLEDGMENTS

It is a pleasure to acknowledge my indebtedness and offer my thanks to a variety of organizations and individuals.

For granting me permission to reprint the contents of the two Metaphor and Irony exhibits and catalogs, I am grateful to the designers and essayists whose work is represented in this book. In particular I thank Ondřej Černy, director, and Olga Plchová, project assistant, Prague Theatre Institute (Divadelní ústav, Praha), for working as my liaisons in acquiring the necessary permissions from the Czech contributors for this publication. The essays by Věra Ptáčková and Marie Zdeňková provide essential perspectives from inside Czech theatre culture, and I thank them for sharing their insights.

Metaphor and Irony exhibition co-curator Helena Albertová deserves my special thanks. She was instrumental in selecting and acquiring the designs that comprised the two exhibits. Her knowledge of both the collected materials of her country's deceased designers and the continuing contributions of contemporary theatre artists enriched our efforts and served as an ongoing tutorial in Czech culture. Many of her colleagues at the Prague Theatre Institute worked on the exhibits and deserve thanks, among them Marie Kmochová and Michaela Chlíbcová. The staff of the International Section of the Prague Theatre Institute also provided helpful and timely assistance, particularly Don Nixon, Sodja Lotker, and the oft retired yet seemingly ever present Jarmila Gabrielová.

This project could not have initially been realized without the interest and support of American exhibitors, the original sponsors and collaborators in my efforts to bring Czech theatre design to audiences in the United States. The first Metaphor and Irony exhibit was partially funded and logistically organized through the auspices of the Ohio Arts Council. I would like to thank them and all the following institutions and individuals: for the Ohio Arts Council, Wayne Lawson, director, and Mary Gray, Riffe Gallery coordinator; for Ohio State University at Columbus, Judith Koroscik, former dean of the College of the Arts, Leslie Ferris, former chair of the Department of Theatre, and Nena Couch, curator of the Jerome Lawrence and Robert E. Lee Theatre Research Institute; for Ohio State University at Lima, former dean Violet Meek; for the Marion Koogler McNay Museum of Art, William Chiego, director, and Linda Hardberger, former curator of the Tobin Gallery; and for the University of Kansas Spencer Museum of Art, Delbert Unruh, former chair, Department of Theatre and Film.

The shipping, crating, framing, and insuring of Metaphor and Irony 2 were completed at my home campus, Ohio State University at Lima. This was a formidable task and I am especially grateful to my colleagues for their efforts: Beverly Bletstein, shipping and insurance; Brad Steinmetz, crating; and Loo and Daniel Brandesky, framing and packing. Other institutions and individuals who deserve thanks for this exhibit include Dean John Snyder for Ohio State University at Lima; for Bowling Green State University's Fine Art Center, Jacqui Nathan, gallery director; for the University of Toledo's Studio Theatre Gallery, James Hill, exhibit preparator, and Sue Ott Rowlands, former chair of the Department of Theatre at Toledo; for Ohio State University at Columbus, Dean Karen Bell, College of the Arts, Leslie Ferris, former chair of the Department of Theatre, Prudence Gill, Hopkins Hall Gallery director, Gayle Strege, curator of the Gladys Keller Snowden Gallery, and Nena Couch, curator of the Lawrence and Lee Theatre Research Institute; for the McNay Museum of Art, William Chiego, director, and Jody Blake, curator of the Tobin Gallery; for the University of the Incarnate Word's Semmes Gallery, Margaret Mitchell; and for the World Bank Art Program, Marina Galvani, director. I offer my sincere gratitude to all.

Developing and producing foreign projects requires travel grants, and I have been fortunate to be supported by several sources. I owe many thanks to my former and current OSU at Lima deans, Violet Meek and John Snyder, respectively, and to associate deans Philip Heath and Michael Cunningham, as well as to my campus research committee. I would also like to thank Halina Stephan, director of the OSU Slavic Center for recent support of my trips to Prague.

Thanks are also due to the OSU Slavic Center and the Tobin Theatre Fund for grants in support of the development of the CD for this book. The two individuals responsible for the programming and layout of the digital images have my great thanks: Brad Steinmetz for devising the overall layout and supervising the CD project and Hannah Rosner for writing code, scanning additional images, and editing drafts.

Many individuals have assisted me over the years in both obvious and subtle ways. Leslie Ferris, my former chair at OSU, agreed to sign an agreement between the theatre department and the theatre section of the Academy of Performing Arts, Prague (DAMU). Her encouragement was and is very much appreciated and has done much to keep me focused on Czech theatre–related projects. Her successor as chair, Mark Shanda, continues to support these projects, for which I am very grateful. I thank Tom Postlewait for patiently listening to my idea for this book and agreeing to help publish it. Maria Ignatieva, my colleague on the Russian projects and OSU at Lima co-worker, has been a welcome supporter through the years, providing advice and insights, particularly on the issues of international project development. Many thanks are due to Delbert Unruh and Dennis Christilles at the University of Kansas. Their contributions to American scholarship on Czech theatre design, both in this book and in essays published in *Theatre Design and Technology*, provided inspiration and, coupled with Jarka Burian's books, a window into Czech theatre culture.

Conversations and collaborations with Czech designers and theatre artists have informed this work in many ways. Petr Matásek, head of the Alternative and Puppet Theatre at DAMU, helped me see the interpenetration of alternative approaches in contemporary theatre design practices. Marketa Fantová, a DAMU-educated designer working in the United States and granddaughter of František Tröster, has provided invaluable insights into the working practices of Czech professional theatres. Milada Pravdová served as managing editor for the Metaphor and Irony 2 catalog and helped shepherd it through publication in Prague. Many other Czech colleagues deserve my thanks, but probably none more than Jaroslav Malina. In the four productions he has designed on campuses of Ohio State University, everyone involved has been the beneficiary of his talent, perspective, and goodwill. In conversations too numerous to recount we have discussed many of the central issues found in this book. The times we have worked together as director and designer have had a significant and beneficial effect on my continuing efforts to understand and explicate Czech theatre from my distant perch in Ohio.

Finally, I would like to thank my Moravian Czech family, past and present, for passing on the seeds of culture and history that have sprouted in the form of this book. I reserve my greatest thanks for my wife, Loo, and son, Daniel. I thank Loo for her care and taste in framing and hanging the Metaphor and Irony 2 exhibit and Daniel for serving enthusiastically as my companion on several trips to Prague. To both, you have my great appreciation for your patience and support.

CZECH THEATRE DESIGN IN THE TWENTIETH CENTURY

■ ■ ■

JOSEPH BRANDESKY

Sources of the Czech Design Legacy

■ ■ ■

The Czech Republic, bordered by Poland, Germany, Slovakia, and Austria, lies literally at the crossroads of Europe. This geographic location explains in part the richness and variety of cultural activities in Prague and the other main cities of the republic. Prague first became an important European capitol during the fourteenth-century reign of the Holy Roman Emperor Charles (Karel) IV. In addition to the many building projects and political alliances that he initiated, he established a university bearing his name, the first in central Europe, in 1348. By the early fifteenth century a Catholic priest and rector of Charles University, Jan Hus, began preaching about the abuses of the church. He advocated reforms that drew many followers and thus the ire of the pope in Rome. Eventually Hus was given safe passage to a council at Constance to air his concerns. Instead, he was questioned and asked to recant. Hus would not recant and was summarily stripped of his priesthood, expelled from the church, and burned at the stake on 6 July 1415. His death signaled the beginning of the Reformation in Bohemia and with it fifty years of the Hussite wars. The centrality of the Czech nation to European geography led to many struggles with powerful neighbors over a variety of political, religious, and economic issues. In response to these and other calamities, the Czech people developed a strong sense of irony, frequently self-deprecating, that grew to permeate the national consciousness.

Irony, metaphor, and a mighty sense of humor, however dark or sardonic, proved necessary as survival traits for a people who, between 1526 and 1918, witnessed the diminution of their national identity by Counter-Reformation forces and, ultimately, Habsburg rulers.[1] This Austrian dynasty's domination of central Europe ended when the region was confirmed as Czechoslovakia at the Treaty of Versailles: thus began the First Republic. American president Woodrow Wilson contributed to the process of building the Czechoslovak nation; the street at the head of

Wenceslas Square (Vaclavské náměstí) just below the National Museum is Wilson Street (Wilsonová ulice). The First Republic had barely begun to develop when the appeasement of Hitler via the Munich Agreement of 1938 ended twenty years of independence. A Nazi "protectorate" was established for Bohemia and Moravia (the Czech homeland) while Slovakia, which resisted the formation of a Czechoslovak state in 1918, was given its independence at the price of becoming a puppet regime.

After the virtual elimination of the Czech Jewish population during World War II, democracy in the form of a reunified Czechoslovakia returned in 1945–48, the period known as the Second Republic. Although American forces under General George Patton were in the country, previous agreements between Roosevelt, Stalin, and Churchill at Yalta gave the Soviet army the honor of liberating Prague from the Nazis. By 1948 a communist-led Czech government with strong ties to the Soviet Union had dismantled many of the democratic practices enjoyed by the preceding republics. After Czechoslovakia was occupied by Soviet troops in August 1968 in response to the perceived threat of the relative freedoms of the Prague Spring, Czechs would not truly rule themselves again for twenty-one years. It was during this time that a young student, Jan Palach, emulated the sacrifice of Jan Hus by setting himself afire at the feet of the equestrian statue of Wenceslas.

The years between 1968 and 1989 were variously referred to as the period of "normalization" or "stagnation." It was a time of repression, disappearances, and acts of social and moral courage. One such act was the signing of Charter 77 by Vaclav Havel and other prominent artists. Havel spent years in prison for this and other acts of civil disobedience. The splintering of the Soviet empire and its satellites, including Czechoslovakia, began with Mikhail Gorbachev's attempts to restructure communism (*perestroika*) and open discourse (*glasnost*'). The process began with peaceful student marches to Wenceslas Square in July 1989 to commemorate Jan Palach's sacrifice. Initial state overreaction and interference quickly escalated to mass marches and civil unrest. But instead of the expected bloodbath, the government quickly collapsed.

The aftermath of the Velvet Revolution of 1989, so called because of the relatively nonviolent transition from communist satellite to independent democracy, posed challenges to the Czech people, not only to accommodate new economic realities but also because of the financial temptations offered by Western standards and aesthetics. The earliest stages of the revolution had taken place in Prague theatres with dissident playwright Vaclav Havel as one of its primary voices. Havel became the leader of the Civic Forum movement and a trusted figurehead for democratic ideals. His suffering under the previous regime added legitimacy to his campaign and led to his election as president of Czechoslovakia.

Theatre occupied a special place in Czech society during the nineteenth and twentieth centuries.[2] German was the language of the Habsburg Empire in political, economic, military, and artistic endeavors. The Czech language and culture were officially submerged. Sunday performances of theatre in Czech were however allowed in Prague, and in the countryside access to native language and culture was found in public puppet performances, these were also allowed periodically in Prague on temporary stages erected in marketplaces. Called *bouda* ("temporary hut" in Czech), these performances maintained the rich Czech folk culture and offered a place for people to congregate. Given the religious upheavals of prior centuries, it was not surprising that Czechs depended on theatres, rather than churches, as institutions of national identity.

The National Revival movement was an attempt by Czechs to assert greater influence, achieve higher status, and restore native culture from within the Habsburg government. Though some progress was made, real change occurred only after the end of World War I in 1918. One success of the Czech National Revival was the construction of the National Theatre, funded by the Czech people. The cornerstone was laid in 1868, but the theatre did not open until 1881. Six months later, the theatre burned to the ground. Another campaign to rally popular support paid for rebuilding efforts, and the National Theatre opened for the final time in 1883. The basement of the theatre features a collection of stones engraved with the names of the cities, towns, and villages that supported the construction financially. The display includes stones from Chicago and other American cities, reflecting the importance of the project in the imagination of Czech émigrés. The motto embossed in the proscenium arch above the stage indicates the relationship between the building and its builders: *Narod Sobě* (The Nation to Itself).

The building of the National Theatre by the Czech people and the elevation of a dissident playwright to president are linked by the importance of theatre to twentieth-century Czech culture. Between these two singular events, Czech audiences benefited from the cosmopolitan openness of the First Republic and suffered under the repressive strategies of the Nazis and the Soviets. Historical realities and cultural trends merged in the formation of theatre design aesthetics in the Czech nation. The links between history and culture form the sources of the Czech design legacy.

Modern Czech theatre has been influenced by a fascinating, sometimes bizarre range of national and international factors, ranging from the natural geography of forests and rivers to puppetry, from cemeteries to holy mountains, from the legends of the golem to the architecture of Prague. Indeed, my own sense of some of the significant influences on visual artists in the Czech Republic is derived from several years of observation in the country, not necessarily in the theatres, and contact with practicing designers. We can discover in the visual signs, codes, and symbols of Czech design for stage and costumes a rich heritage of folk culture and beliefs. At the same time, operating alongside this heritage, the major movements of premodern and modern European art have been essential. Moreover, the visual artists of the theatre are, in many cases, not just people of the theatre but established painters, sculptors, and architects. They are, with hardly an exception, highly intelligent in their approach to theatre. To an outsider their methods may appear opaque, yet one can begin to ascertain the sources of their artistic perspectives by an examination of the many visual referents embedded in the Czech homeland.

At first glance the Czech countryside appears to be dominated by agricultural production. Indeed, the land is fertile and productive to the point of self-sufficiency, a factor which is a source of pride for the nation but poses new challenges for its future as a member of the European Union. The country has several low, forested mountain ranges with rivers that flow through the valleys. Bohemia and Moravia are blessed with many beautiful natural features that have drawn city dwellers away from the capitol cities of Prague and Brno for centuries. Numerous castles, chateaus, and lodges built by aristocrats in former periods attest to the popularity of the countryside.

Just north of Prague is the mountain called Řip, the place where legend describes a nomadic Slavic tribe led by a man called Čech who proclaimed a new homeland in his name. It is a place tied to national identity and, not surprisingly, was depicted in numerous paintings and stories in the nineteenth century as a part of the National Revival movement. Near the southern boundary of Bohemia, snowmelt and runoff from the Šumava mountains give birth to the Vltava River (Moldau in

German). While its headwaters are a charming mountain stream, the river widens on its way north to Prague and, after moving beyond that city, joins the Labe River. Across the border in Germany, the same river becomes the Elbe and makes its way to the Baltic Sea.

These and many other mountains, forests, and rivers inspired a rich legacy of folk tales. Superstitions, pagan beliefs, and the wildness and relative isolation of the countryside led to stories about water nymphs and witches along with heroes aided by creatures with powers of supernatural proportions. In the nineteenth century many of the stories were collected and retold by Božena Nemcová (1820–1862) and Karel Jaromir Erben (1811–1870). Perhaps the best-known use of these stories was the retelling of one of Erben's tales by Antonín Dvořák in his opera *Rusalka* (The Water Goblin). Before the publication of the tales and their incorporation by composers and others into "legitimate" forms, Czech folk tales were frequently told through puppet performances. The popularity of these performances was enormous and helped preserve national identity, thus serving not only as both education and entertainment but also as a vital reservoir of national memory and identity. A key aspect of puppet theatre is an open theatricalism, wherein audiences accept that the figures they watch are being manipulated by plainly visible performers.

The openly acknowledged devices used in popular puppet theatre— the mixture of scales (the combination of different sizes of an object or person), the simultaneous appearance of animate and inanimate performers, direct address and other deliberately nonrealistic techniques— laid the groundwork for twentieth-century Czech theatre artists. Directors and designers were drawn to nonrealistic methods of stage production, knowing that their audiences had been conditioned by the legacy of puppetry. For example, it is not unusual to view a puppet production that features three or more representations of a given character. A character may be depicted with a marionette, then with a large-scale version of the character's head or arm, then as a full-size mannequin: mixed scale is used to amplify, reduce, or juxtapose characters in emotional or dramatic situations. This principle was adapted for use in traditional theatre productions by Czech designers.

Productions that illustrate the use of mixed scale in this volume include designs by Vlastislav Hofman, František Tröster, and Josef Svoboda. Hofman mixed actors with oversize painted images in his 1920 design for *The Tempest* (fig. 1, HOFM03) to illustrate the magical nature of Prospero's island. Mysterious giant figures in the background of his

1. HOFM03. Vlastislav Hofman's design for *The Tempest*, directed by Karel Hugo Hilar, Vinohrady Theatre, 1920.

rendering dwarfed the figures of Trinculo, Stefano, and Caliban. František Tröster also employed the puppet device of mixed scale as a cornerstone of design methodology. Tröster's signature monumental or hyperbolic style characterizes his 1936 designs for *Julius Caesar* and *The Inspector General*. The raised hoof of an oversize Roman equestrian statue hovers over the action in the former (fig. 2, TROS10). The actors are literally under the abstracted hoof, a visual amplification of the bloody activities occurring below. On the other hand, the inebriated condition of Khlestakov and the Mayor in *The Inspector General* is accentuated by a set of large declined and slanted panels that move as the characters attempt to enter a room (TROS01). Finally, Josef Svoboda, one of Tröster's pupils, frequently used oversize projected images in his Laterna Magika productions. This predilection is also easily seen in a production photo from his 1978 design for *Tristan und Isolde* (fig. 3, SVOB01) wherein the title characters are depicted in the midst of clouds and sky.

A more straightforward use of puppet techniques is visible in the playful 2002 costume designs by Helena Anýžová for *Paris Plays First Fiddle*

2. TROS10. Production photo of František Tröster's "monumental" design for *Julius Caesar*, directed by Jiří Frejka, National Theatre, 1936. Photo by Alexander Paul.

(fig. 4, ANYZ02; ANZY03, ANZY04, ANZY05). Her sketches indicate that the costumes are not merely dressing for the actors, but that they are meant to be manipulated in performance. Petra Štětinová Goldflamová was a pupil at the Alternative and Puppet Theatre section of the Academy of Performing Arts in Prague (DAMU), and her costume designs reflect this training. Each of her renderings, though designed for actors, suggests visual aspects, codes, and features of the formal design and movement of puppets. This is especially true for her 2002 designs for *Matthew the Honest* (fig. 5, STET03; STET04). The figures are drawn without regard for natural human proportions; rather, they suggest singular characteristics. The faces resemble stylized masks and lead viewers to conclusions as to the

3. SVOBO1. Projections, lighting effects, and scenery combine in Josef Svoboda's design for *Tristan und Isolde*, Grand Theatre, Geneva, 1978.

nature of the characters in the same way that puppets do. One of Štětinová's teachers at DAMU, Petr Matásek, spent much of his career at DRAK, one of the premiere puppet theatres in his country, located in Hradec Králové. Naděžda (Hope), the puppet he designed for *Cirkus Unikum* in 1978, was openly manipulated by actors (fig. 6, MATA08; MATA06, MATA07, MATA11). She performed a series of circus acts and, though inanimate, became a living presence onstage through her interaction with the performers. In recent years, Matásek has become a frequent designer in both traditional (National Theatre) and nontraditional (warehouse, public square, crypt) venues. His work has garnered acclaim in his country and internationally. Matásek's work with puppets and alternative theatre techniques is also tied to the Czech design style of the seventies and eighties called action design.

Action design featured three dominant tenets: designs should be functional and malleable with focus given to the performers and their interaction with the set; authentic properties (items from the surroundings, including trash) should be used and misused to provoke metaphorical associations; and open communication with the audience using verbal and nonverbal means should be maintained. The development of these tenets is at least partially attributable to the puppet and popular theatre traditions of metaphor and open communication. Miroslav

4. ANYZ02. One of Helena Anýžová's manipulated costume designs for *Paris Plays First Fiddle*, National Theatre of Moravia and Silesia at Hukvaldy Castle, 2002.

Melena's designs for Studio Ypsilon, including those for *The Twelve Chairs* in 1973 (fig. 7, MELE01), illustrate aspects of this trend. Productions at Studio Y took place in intimate spaces with direct contact between audience and performers. The settings were extremely flexible, malleable, and openly transformed by the actors. Jan Dušek's 1984 design for *Too Loud a Solitude* (fig. 8, DUSE01) clearly indicates the use of authentic materials, as does Jaroslav Malina's 1998 production of *Come Nasce il Soggeto Cinematografico* (fig. 9, MALI07). But Malina's use of

5. STET03. Petra Štětinová Goldflamová's puppet-inspired costume design for the State Spokesman in *Matthew the Honest*, directed by Arnošt Goldflam, Dlouhá Theatre, 2002.

open devices (for example, rope lines in plain view) and mixture of scales (a lushly painted backdrop upstage of the actors) has direct ties to the aesthetics of the puppet theatre. In each of these cases, stage and actor transformations are shared directly with audiences, echoing the simultaneity of real and theatrical experience in puppet performances.

6. MATA08. Production photo showing actors manipulating Petr Matásek's puppet, Naděžda (Hope), during *Cirkus Unikum*, directed by Josef Krofta, Drak Theatre, 1978. Photo by Josef Ptáček.

Yet another impulse is attributable to the visual style called the Czech grotesque. The roots of this impulse are, like puppet theatre, found at the intersection of history and culture. Central Europe, especially the Czech homeland, was the locus of European conflicts—wars and battles—and crises—plagues and epidemics—throughout the ages. In the twentieth century, Czechoslovakia's membership in the Soviet empire's Eastern Bloc brought communist forces to within a few kilometers of western Europe. Before that, occupation and the battles of two world

7. MELE01. Miroslav Melena's malleable, "action" design for
The Twelve Chairs, directed by Jan Schmid, Studio Ypsilon, 1973.

8. DUSE01. Jan Dušek's design for an adaptation of
Bohumil Hrabal's novel, *Too Loud a Solitude*, directed by
Evald Schorm, Theatre on the Balustrade, 1984.

9. MALI07. "Action" and painterly devices mark
Jaroslav Malina's design for *Come Nasce il Soggeto Cinematografico*,
directed by Ivan Balad'a, Municipal Theatre in Zlín, 1998.

wars had been fought in and around Bohemia and Moravia. Earlier still,
Napoleon left his mark in 1805 at the battle of Austerlitz (Slavkov na
Brna) near Brno, where the French army decisively defeated the combined forces of the Russians and Austrians and opened a path to Poland
and points east.

But perhaps the most significant battle for Czechs was lost in 1620 at
White Mountain in the early stages of the Thirty Years' War. A contingent
comprised of Protestant Czech estates was defeated by the Catholic Habsburg army, thus ending the struggle of Reformation forces that had
begun earlier by followers of the religious iconoclast and martyr Jan Hus.
Czech aristocrats lost their property to Austrians and Germans, who
enforced an adherence to the German language, in place of Czech, and to

the primacy of the Roman Catholic Church. The Counter-Reformation brought a countrywide building program of Baroque churches. Each of these new churches, *kostel* in Czech, clearly resembled a castle or fortress; in addition to their function as bastions of Catholic ideology, they were defensible sites built to withstand possible conflicts with recalcitrant Protestant forces. Most villages and towns still have a *kostel*, though some were converted to secular purposes during the communist years. Many have graveyards nearby or directly adjacent, and the remembrances to the dead found in or near these churches lead to a clear understanding of the grotesque.

The plague was an unwelcome visitor to the Czech lands in previous centuries. Thousands died and were memorialized in plague columns, impressive structures that traditionally occupied squares in villages throughout Europe and featured artists' renditions of the bones of the deceased, capped with a crucifix. They symbolized the Christian belief in the sometimes agonizing transition from earthly life ("Remember man you are dust and to dust you shall return . . . ") to heavenly salvation. The rather grotesque appearance of these reminders of our mortality is all the more jolting when they are placed in the center of village life where one cannot avoid contact with their visual codes and messages.

Nowhere are the grisly depictions of the aftermath of plague and war in the Czech lands more evident than in the famed Kostnice in the village of Sedlec.[3] Originally part of a Cistercian monastery, the cemetery adjoining All Saints Church (Kostel Všech Svatých) had been in constant use since the thirteenth century. It accumulated the remains of victims of plague and of both the Hussite wars and the Thirty Years' War. Eventually the powerful aristocratic Schwartzenberg family purchased the property and, in 1870, hired František Rint to bring artistic order to approximately forty thousand human skeletons. The results include an oversize coat of arms, chandeliers, pyramids, and many other objects composed almost completely of human bones. Despite the presence of paintings of saints framed with baroque figures made of mother-of-pearl, the space is dominated by constructions like the seven-foot-tall obelisk-shaped candleholder filled with human skulls and topped by a fleshy, fully colored sculpture of an angel. The vault that houses Rint's creations is comprised of assemblages that combine the Gothic and the Baroque, the religious and the secular, the mysterious and the quotidian.

Czech artists and audiences clearly display an understanding and appreciation for the contradictions embedded in images inspired by the grotesque. They have become an integral part of Czech culture, both high and low. For example, no visitor to Prague can avoid a constant barrage of images printed on clothing, hats, books, and elsewhere concerning the legend of the golem. The story begins in the sixteenth century when the leader of the Jewish community in Prague, Rabbi Loew, had a dream telling him how to construct a being from clay. This being, the golem, would protect Jews from anti-Semitic mobs.[4] The formula for animating the golem consisted of alchemical and mystical preparations, culminating in the insertion of a *Schem* (a parchment inscribed with the name of God) into the mouth of the clay creature. The golem could pass for a man but could not speak. According to legend, it eventually became uncontrollable and had to be destroyed.

If Rabbi Loew and the golem represent the nexus of religion and the occult for Jews, then Faust is the representative of this impulse for Christians. The Czech filmmaker Jan Švankmajer cleverly combined aspects of the Faust and golem stories in his 1994 film *The Faust Lesson* (*Lekce Faust*).[5] Building on the popularity and familiarity of both the Faust and the golem stories, the film is an extension of a longstanding tradition for staging the grotesque. The Faust legend in particular has provided the impetus for many puppet and stage productions in years past and remains a nearly constant presence on Czech stages. In 2001, for example, Petr Matásek designed two versions of the Faust legend (Goethe's and Marlowe's); one utilized puppet techniques, the other was staged in Gorlice, a vault under Vyšehrad, the Gothic seat of the Bohemian kings.[6] Václav Havel's updated version of the Faust story, *Temptation* (*Pokoušení*), written in 1985, has been produced many times in the Czech Republic and abroad. A production directed by Charles Marowitz at the Estates Theatre ended an eighteen-month run in December 2005. The sets and costumes were designed by two artists represented in this book, David Marek and Jana Zbořilová, respectively. Ivo Žídek's set design for a 1991 production of *Temptation* (fig. 10, ZIDE01) was directed by Jan Grossman at the Theatre on the Balustrade and followed their 1990 collaboration on Havel's *Largo Desolato* (ZIDE02).

The action of *Temptation* takes place in a nameless institute where Dr. Foustka has begun to research forbidden alchemical subjects. Foustka performs incantations in his apartment and "summons" an unpleasant man named Fistula, a playful abbreviation of Mephistopheles, who may or may not be a devil. The space of the play requires both a familiar ordinariness and the potential for metaphysical transformations. Žídek's

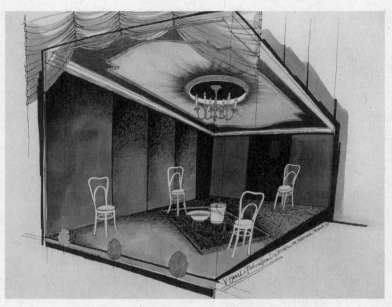

10. ZIDE01. Ivo Žídek's seemingly ordinary setting for
Václav Havel's version of Faust, *Temptation*, directed by Jan Grossman,
Theatre on the Balustrade, 1991.

biography (in the biographies toward the end of this book) describes his approach to the problem of space in this play and provides an example of the multilayered approach typical of late twentieth-century Czech designers: "The central accent of the stage design . . . was a round opening in an expressively angled ceiling under which were placed a bucket and a washbasin. It served as a passage for raids by the devil and was at the same time an ordinary, uncomfortable hole, through which water dripped—a clear use of metaphor and irony."

The simplicity of Žídek's design for the setting of *Temptation* was at least partially due to the small stage of the Theatre on the Balustrade, while Dana Hávová's costume designs for a 1990 production of the play (fig. 11, HAV001; HAV002–10) illustrate both the ordinary everyday dress of characters from the nameless institute and its transformation during the witches' Sabbath finale of the play. Her depiction of the characters also retains an aspect of grotesque caricature in both street dress and fantastic costume.

The sources of the Czech grotesque for theatre designers are hidden in plain sight. They are visible in the many Baroque churches, cemeteries, and monuments to the dead. Over the centuries these images have

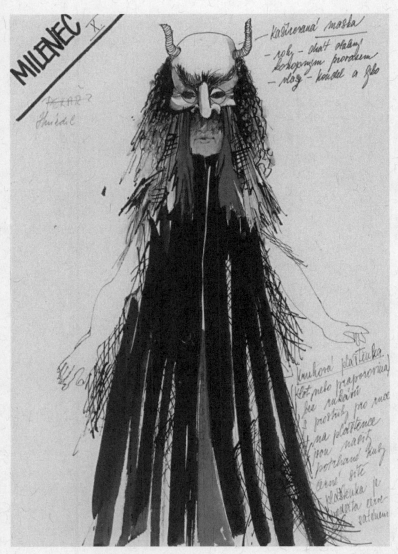

11. HAVOO1. Devilish partygoer costume by Dana Hávová for *Temptation*, directed by Jan Burian, Tyl Theatre, 1990.

been integrated into paintings, sculptures, and buildings. Their ubiquity suggests perhaps the most obvious source of visual material for theatre designers in Prague: its architecture.

Prague's elevation to architectural greatness began with the Gothic constructions of the Přemyslid dynasty, notably at their fortress above the Vltava, Vyšehrad. The current castle district, Hradčany, including Saint

Vitus Cathedral, was begun in the ninth century and completed in the nineteenth century on a promontory above Lesser Town (Mala Straná) on the western bank of the Vltava. Nearby, the romanesque church of Saint George provides a clear contrast to the French neo-Gothic west façade of Saint Vitus. In this same district one can see many Baroque buildings, some featuring *sgraffito* designs. Across the fifteenth-century Charles Bridge to the center of Old Town, Baroque, Renaissance, and art nouveau buildings dominate the view, but architecture from other, later periods can be seen as well. Beyond this square on the way to the Louis XVI–inspired Estates Theatre (1781–1783) one passes the Black Madonna House (1911–1912), the prime exemplar of the Museum of Czech Cubism it houses. In short, nearly all periods of architectural development are visible in the streets of Prague, providing designers endless opportunities to represent and transform historical details in their stage designs. The fabled beauty of Prague affected Adolph Hitler, who refrained from bombing the city and reportedly planned to live there when war ended. The visual splendor and variety of the city indisputably guides and sanctions those capable of absorbing inspiration from their surroundings. Perhaps it is not surprising, then, that many of the best twentieth-century Czech theatre designers were architects and painters.

The Czech affiliation among architects, artists, and theatre designers begins early in the twentieth century and continues to this day. Bedřich Feuerstein (1892–1936) was trained as an architect and distinguished himself as a stage designer in Prague during the twenties and thirties. His design for the 1921 premiere of Karel Čapek's *RUR* at the National Theatre appears on the cover of Jarka Burian's *Modern Czech Theatre*.[7] Feuerstein's contemporary, Vlastislav Hofman, achieved great fame as an architect and designer during the years of the First Republic. Hofman's designs display a keen appreciation for the expressionist and cubist features prevalent during this period. The tendencies are especially clear in his collaborations with the director Karel Hugo Hilar (1885–1935) at the National and Vinohrady theatres (HOFM01–03).

By the midthirties another architect-designer, František Tröster, had formed a close working relationship with an influential director, Jiří Frejka (1904–1952). Frejka was particularly interested in nontraditional staging techniques and avant-garde approaches to theatre. In Tröster he found a kindred spirit. This creative duo was responsible for many great productions at the National Theatre, including *The Inspector General*

(TROS01) and *Julius Caesar* (TROS10) in 1936 and *Romeo and Juliet* (TROS05) in 1937. František Tröster taught another generation of theatre artists with strong interests in architecture and interior design, including Josef Svoboda and Miroslav Melena. Svoboda was Tröster's student at the Central School of Interior Design. Melena studied with Tröster at DAMU and has devoted his attention to theatre architecture in recent years. David Marek, also a DAMU graduate, describes himself as a designer of settings and interiors. His 1994 design for Goethe's *Clavigo* (MARE04) was inspired by the cubist figures made popular on Czech stages by Hofman earlier in the century.

More than a few of the best twentieth-century Czech designers were well known, not as architects but as skilled artists. Their painterly preferences spanned the gamut of modernist trends. Once again Prague artists benefited from their geographical placement in Europe as art movements from East and West met in the center. Symbolist, cubist, and surrealist influences came from Paris while futurist and constructivist ideas arrived from Moscow. Secessionist and expressionist principles crossed the nearby borders from Vienna and Berlin. In all cases, Czech artists absorbed and transformed these movements for their own purposes. Of the many painters who made contributions to theatre design, Alfons Mucha (1860–1939) was one of the first. He is famous for his art nouveau contributions to painting and the applied arts (especially his posters for Sarah Bernhardt), and early in his career he worked as a scene painter and occasional set designer. (In this regard he has much in common with the early twentieth-century Russian painter-designers who worked for Sergei Diagilev's *Ballets Russes*, for example, Léon Bakst, Boris Anisfeld, and Nikolai Rerich.)

A more deliberate overlap between serious painters and stage design can be seen in the career of Josef Čapek (1897–1945). Čapek's paintings and drawings variously display the influence of primitivism (from Henri Rousseau), folk art (from Mikhail Larionov), and cubism. In 1912 he made his second trip to Paris, accompanied by Vlastislav Hofman, intent on studying cubist art.[8] Aspects of these influences can be seen in Čapek's sets and costumes for the 1922 National Theatre premiere of *The Insect Comedy*.

Several Czech artists made occasional appearances as designers in the middle of the century. Jan Zrzavý (1890–1977), an artist tied to symbolism, designed *Idomeneo* (1931) and *Lohengrin* (1940) at the National Theatre. František Tichý (1896–1961) had a lifetime fascination with circus performers, especially clowns. From the late twenties through the forties Tichý designed sporadically for the Švanda and National Theatres. Expressionism, cubism, and abstractionism were the hallmarks of Jan Sládek's work. He eventually made his way to Prague and worked at the Vinohrady and National Theatres before founding the Realistic Theatre after the end of World War II. His career began at the National Theatre of Moravia in Ostrava where he executed beautiful renderings for *The Merchant of Venice* (SLAD01) in 1933 and *Antony and Cleopatra* (fig. 12, SLAD02) in 1938.

Sládek was joined in a long career as a designer and painter by František Muzika (1900–1974), who is best known for the lyrical surrealism of his later years, although he began working in the theatre in 1927. "At the beginning of his career, he was influenced by [the] Soviet avant-garde example, and built on Constructivism, refining its austerity by lyrical or shrewdly playful elements. In the 1930s and 1940s his stage design became very close to the art of painting. Dreamlike surrealist worlds mingled into both fields of the artist's work. The motives in his paintings appear in his scenography and vice versa (the profile of a girl, the Moon, shells, palms, antique torsos)."[9]

After 1945 Muzika was appointed professor of applied painting and graphics at the Prague School of Applied Arts. At approximately the same time, Otakar Schindler studied monumental painting at the same institution. Helena Albertová's monograph on Schindler is subtitled *Stage Designer and Painter* (1999), and the examples of painting it contains verify the same line of interconnectedness found in Muzika's work. Schindler's designs for the 1974 production of *The Wood Demon* (SCHI01) and the 1980 production of *All's Well That Ends Well* (fig. 13, SCHI02) are particularly reminiscent of his painting. The design for *The Wood Demon* (directed by Jan Kačer) reduces the Russian setting to a handful of items: a straw-filled buggy, a wooden bench, a blanket on the ground with a lamp on a stool nearby, all framed within a faded gold arch. The color palette is limited to blacks, grays, browns, and some gold highlights. It is an abstract setting worthy of Chekhov's tragicomedy. The dilapidated, cracked appearance of the walls in *All's Well That Ends Well* is similarly monochromatic, except for the vividly bloodstained wall on stage right, evidently the site of a shooting or a firing squad. An added advantage for us to understand Schindler's design process was his penchant for including storyboards that traced the visual development of the setting from start to finish.

12. SLAD02. Expressionism and cubism are evident in
Jan Sládek's design for *Antony and Cleopatra*, directed by Jan Škoda,
National Theatre of Moravia and Silesia, 1938.

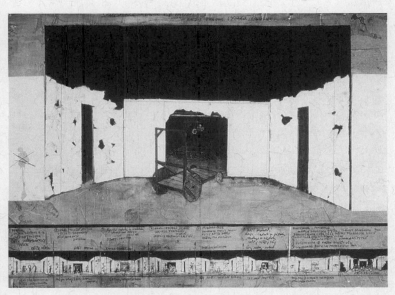

13. SCH102. Detailed storyboards vividly display the development
of Otakar Schindler's design for *All's Well That Ends Well*, directed
by Jiří Fréhar, Drama Theatre of Hradec Králové, 1980.

Jaroslav Malina is one of the most active designer-painters currently working in the Czech Republic. A 1999 monograph on Malina lists twenty one-person exhibitions. He has also participated in over thirty group exhibitions. In December 2004 a career retrospective exhibition was held in Liberec that featured 154 paintings, design renderings, posters, and ceramics. The quotation used as the title of the chapter devoted to Malina in Tony Davis's 2001 book *Stage Design* says it all: "There is a permanent interaction between my painting and my design."[10] In 1955 he began to study painting privately with Zdeněk Sklenář (1910–1986), a contemporary and friend of František Muzika. Malina's 1988 design for *Miss Julie* (MAL110) brings the lush colors of Midsummer Eve into the kitchen. A metaphorical river of blood runs through the space while, above it all, Cupid prepares to loose his arrows. In the words of Malina: "The distinctive qualities of my work are my use of color, my sense, or feeling, of spatial proportion, my use of materials and structures, my emotionality, my visual mystery and my ability to balance on the edge between rationality and emotionality, authenticity and stylization."[11] Another example of the "visual mystery" which can be linked to his painting style is his 2003 rendering for *A Lynx's Hour* (MAL102–03). The spare design for a simple wall is the anchor for the painted stars above it. Malina's work on stage and at the easel continues and extends the legacy of twentieth-century Czech painter-designers. It is too early to tell whether this tradition will find younger adherents in the new century.

The stage designs of these architects and painters and their colleagues led Halina Stephan to remark that "Czech audiences learned about Modernism at the theatre, not in galleries."[12] Twentieth-century Czech audiences lived in a culture with historical architecture preserved in both urban and rural settings, as well as a tradition of repeating and performing folk stories through puppetry. They saw modernist trends extended to the stage by talented designers. The rich heritage of the Czech visual lexicon is the subject of this book.

The essays which form the body of this volume were originally commissioned for the exhibition catalogs. Length restrictions at that time resulted in the condensation of some of the original essays, and the full texts have been restored here. Each of the essayists examines Czech design from a unique and enlightening perspective.

Věra Ptáčková is one of the preeminent Czech theatre-design scholars and serves on the faculty of Fine Arts and Theatre at Masaryk University in Brno, Czech Republic. Her essay, "Trends in Twentieth-Century Czech Theatre Design," thoughtfully links designers from the first exhibit to the mannerist legacy of Giuseppe Arcimboldo.[13] Her historical insights are particularly interesting for provoking associations between theatre design and the various art movements covered before and during the span of the first Metaphor and Irony exhibit.

Dennis P. Christilles, associate professor of theatre and film at the University of Kansas, describes the background of Czech scenographic practices and its influence in the United States from the perspective of a designer and scholar. His essay, "Czech Scenography in America," establishes the link between the so-called Prague school of semiotics and stage design and production techniques.[14] As an example of this link, Christilles describes the Czech use of stage design as "the other actor" in a production.

The third essay, "Modernism to Imagism," is contributed by designer and eminent Czech design scholar Delbert Unruh, professor of theatre and film at the University of Kansas. As the title suggests, the essay spans the major art movements affecting twentieth-century Czech designers.[15] In the section on modernism, Unruh describes František Tröster's influence on Czech design as equal to that of Robert Edmond Jones's in the United States.

Marie Zdeňková, head of the scenography section at the Theatre Institute, Prague, provides the final essay, "Authority, Playfulness, Metaphor, and Irony." She traces the connections between those who came before František Tröster and those who have come after.[16] The background of Tröster's career provided by Zdeňková is particularly helpful in developing a context for his contributions to Czech theatre.

I include two appendixes in this book: the designers' biographies and a list of the images found on the CD. The former prepared substantially by Helena Albertová, includes the designer information originally printed in the exhibition catalogs. Some listings have been updated or amended since that first publication. The latter includes the performance information and the identification system used to locate a specific image on the disk. Any reproduction of a design in the print edition of the book will consistently use the specific codes found on this list. It should also be noted that the text from the printed edition is also available on the disk with clickable links to the included images.

Finally, twenty-seven designers were represented in the two Metaphor and Irony exhibits. Among them are many of the best twentieth-century

Czech theatre designers. Nevertheless, some artists of note were not included.[17] Two issues determined the selections made by the exhibit co-curators: availability of museum-quality items and cost restrictions related to the size of the exhibits. Despite these limitations, the images and essays included here supply ample evidence of the consistent quality and creativity of Czech stage and costume designers in the twentieth century.

NOTES

1. The history of central Europe and the Czech nation can be found in numerous volumes. Two that are particularly helpful are A. H. Hermann's *A History of the Czechs* and E. Garrison Walters's *The Other Europe: Eastern Europe to 1945*. The former describes the geographical importance of the Czech people in central Europe while the latter clarifies the place of the Czechs regarding neighboring countries.

2. Jarka Burian provides an excellent digest of Czech theatre history from 1780 through 1999 in *Modern Czech Theatre: Reflector and Conscience of a Nation*.

3. Kostnice is the ossuary located in All Saints Church in the village of Sedlec. The nearby city of Kutná Hora is a former silver-mining and minting center. There are other ossuaries in the Czech Republic, but none more clearly illustrate the grotesque aspects of Baroque Gothic. Details concerning Kostnice can be found in Jan Kulich's text in a pamphlet entitled *The Ossuary* or by visiting the official web site: www.kostnice.cz. This site includes still images and text describing the history of the place as well as a virtual tour of the ossuary. Czech filmmaker Jan Švankmajer made a short film about the ossuary, *Kostnice*, in 1970.

4. Prague had one of the first Jewish communities in central Europe. In A.D. 907 a settlement near Old Town, the historic center of Prague on the east bank of the Vltava River, was given to the Jews. This area, later given the name Josefov, still exists and currently has two working synagogues, but the Jewish population of Prague and Czechoslovakia was virtually annihilated during World War II. There are several readily available sources on the Jewish presence in Prague, among them a pamphlet, *The Prague Golem: Jewish Stories of the Ghetto*.

5. Jan Švankmajer (b. 1934) is a Czech filmmaker, painter, and sculptor. His filmic combination of the Faust and golem legends is set in an alchemist's laboratory. The actor who will eventually play Faust finds a book of spells/formulas and molds a ball of clay into a child. He then inserts a *Schem* into the mouth of the "child" who, through stop-action animation, comes to life. Once the *Schem* is removed, the child reverts to an inanimate state. The film also features puppet performances of the Faust story. Švankmajer's work is laced with a strong sense of the grotesque and the surreal. See Peter Hames's *Dark Alchemy: The Films of Jan Švankmajer* and *Jan Švankmajer: Transmutation of the Senses*, edited by Simeona Hošková and Kveta Otcovská.

6. Petr Matásek's work on the *Faust* production in Gorlice was awarded the Alfréd Radok Prize for best Czech scene design in 2001.

7. Burian includes a section on the premiere of Čapek's best-known play in *Modern Czech Theatre*, 36–38.

8. Biographical information found in Alena Pomajzlová, *Josef Čapek: The Humblest Art*, 183–184.

9. Muzika worked on many designs during his career. His design for Bohuslav Martinu's opera *Julietta*, directed by Jindřich Honzl at the National Theatre in 1938, contains several of the key characteristics described in this quotation. The full biographical entry and a reproduction of the design for *Julietta* is in Helena Albertová, ed., *The Scenographer's Art: Czech Theatre Stage and Costume Design of the Twentieth Century*, 9.

10. The chapter on Jaroslav Malina is in the form of a long interview. There are two paintings, his designs and photos from the film *Magpie in Hand*, and a large selection of designs and photos from productions of the seventies to the nineties. Tony Davis, *Stage Design*, 62–75.

11. Davis, 69.

12. The quote is from Halina Stephan's unpublished comments preceding the opening of the Metaphor and Irony 2 exhibit at the Hopkins Hall Gallery of Ohio State University, 8 November 2005.

13. Věra Ptáčková is one of the most respected observers of Czech and international scene design. Her book on the history of the Prague Quadrennial International Exhibitions of Theatre Design and Architecture, *A Mirror of World Theatre*, is especially noteworthy. Giuseppe Arcimboldo (1527–1593) was a mannerist artist born in Milan. He was appointed a court painter and designer of spectacles for the Habsburg monarchs Ferdinand I and Maximillian II. At the behest of a third Habsburg monarch, Rufolf II, Arcimboldo moved to Prague, where his family was ennobled in 1580. He continued to live and work in Prague until 1587 when he returned to Milan. Good reproductions of Arcimboldo's fanciful paintings and designs can be found in the Taschen series book *Arcimboldo*.

14. The Prague school of structuralist linguistics included Jindřich Honzl (1894–1953), a Czech director who worked with several of the most influential interwar Czech theatre artists, among them Emil František Burian, Jan Werich, and Jiří Voskovec. Dennis Christilles and Delbert Unruh assert that Honzl was the first to use the term "action" in relation to scene design in 1941. For more information on the influence of semiotics on Czech scene design see Christilles and Unruh, "The Semiotics of Action Design."

15. Delbert Unruh is a contributing editor for *Theatre Design and Technology* and has published more than thirty essays on American and European stage design and theory. In 1992 he wrote *Towards a New Theatre: The Lectures of Robert Edmond Jones*, and he recently completed *USITT Presents the Designs of*

Ming Cho Lee. He served on the jury for the 2003 Prague Quadrennial International Exhibition of Theatre Design and Architecture.

16. Zdeňková is a frequent contributor to the Czech journal *Theatre*, published by the Theatre Institute, Prague.

17. Among the pre-WWII designers not represented in *Czech Theatre Design in the Twentieth Century: Metaphor and Irony* are Josef Čapek (1887–1945), František Zelenka (1904–1944), František Muzika (1900–1974), Antonín Heythum (1901–1954), and Bedřich Feuerstein (1892–1936). Contemporary Czech designers not shown here include Daniel Dvořak, Irena Greifová, Zuzana Krejzková, David Cajthaml, and many others. Where possible, the bibliography will direct readers to visual resources for these designers.

■ ■ ■

VĚRA PTÁČKOVÁ

Trends in Twentieth-Century Czech Theatre Design

■ ■ ■

It was no accident that Prague achieved its position as a center of international stage design; traditionally in the Czech lands, the peaks of stage design coincided with the peaks of European art and were connected with the position of Prague as a seat of kings. In the sixteenth century the initiator and organizer of celebrations at the imperial court was the renowned Giuseppe Arcimboldo, painter of bizarre portraits and allegories composed out of plants and animals. Arcimboldo's costume designs turned the dancers into mannerist artifacts through the use of stylized heads and appropriate attributes. At the celebration of the Bohemian Estates in 1617, Prague experienced the first transformation stage north of the Alps; in 1723 Giuseppe Galli-Bibiena built a wooden theatre with Baroque décor for the celebrations around the coronation of Charles VI as king of Bohemia. In the 1780s Prague entered European theatre history with the building of the Nostic Theatre (today the Theatre of the Estates), for which Josef Platzer created a classical décor. European stage design recorded other notable impulses at the end of the nineteenth century—passive existence turned into a creative current which not only adopted impulses from the fine arts, but very soon itself became a source of inspiration.

There were also Czech artists who held their own in the contest for modern expression. In 1910 the director K. H. Hilar took over the Vinohrady Theatre (built in 1907) with a vision of theatre production as composition put together from different elements. His idea was that the stage designer should be a creative partner, chosen on the basis of an affinity of artistic views. He was aware of the possibilities that such a conjunction could open up, and experimented with a number of leading Czech artists before eventually settling on the architect Vlastislav Hofman. The beginnings of modern scenic expression in the Czech lands are generally connected with symbolism and expressionism, which Hilar and Hofman showed in 1919 in a production of *The Hussites*, a historical drama by Arnošt Dvořák. It was staged one month before Leopold Jessner's production of Schiller's *William Tell* in Berlin.

However, Hofman's first set designs show the clear signs of yet another influence—cubism. Hofman belonged to a generation of architects who, in their efforts to achieve a strictly purpose-made style in the context of the modern, reacted by a swing toward concepts in painting and sculpture, of which the strongest inspiration was the Parisian cubism of Picasso and Braque. A group of Prague artists in the twenties were the only ones in the whole of Europe who experimented with the idea of cubist architecture. For the purpose of our theme, it is interesting that the architects of these designs, whether completed or only proposed, include some of the founders of modern Czech stage design: Bedřich Feuerstein, Ladislav Machon, Jiří Kroha—and above all Vlastislav Hofman.

Hofman's first set designs (for *The Hussites*) essentially replicate the Baroque system of painted wings and backcloth. Later, however, he tried out the effectiveness of truly compositional interiors, created from cubist- or constructivist-furnished environments for historical plays. The transparent backcloths for Shakespeare's *Tempest* (HOFM01) evoked the impression of an ever-present dreamlike reality: the basic set remained the same; the changes concerned only details in two communicating acting areas. Verhaeren's symbolist *Dawn* inspired in the Hilar-Hofman partnership an interest in color and in methods of transforming action symbols into dramatic shape. Hofman tended toward exaggeration and symbolic colorfulness, and he formulated the difference between empirical and dramatic reality. His production of *Hamlet* (1926) is an example of the style that Hilar promoted in his final phase: civilism, or *die neue Sachlichkeit* [a new matter-of-factness]. Hofman described the set like this: "A flat stage floor without stairs, almost modern furniture on an enormous scale. Roller screens used for the first time." Even the costumes were conceived as properties—Gertrude and Ophelia were reminiscent of fashionable beauties of the twenties. Hofman's feeling for space was shown at its most striking in his production of Dostoyevsky's *Crime and Punishment* (1928, directed by Jan Bor), where the acting space was divided into a shallow strip in front of the house, where the murder happens; a deep carriageway cutting through the façade of the house; and a view into the room in which the dramatic action takes place. In his designs for *Macbeth* (1939, directed by Jan Bor) he changed, according to the locality, the height and proportions of a portalled opening, through which the suggestion of Gothic architecture was again complemented by contemporary furniture. Hofman's work developed from the direct application of visual motifs and styles all the way to the subordination of visual criteria to dramatic requirements; its primary meaning consisted of this shift. He established set design as a creative element of the dramatic work with equal rights.

The generation of the thirties and European cultural climate was confronted with communism and fascism. Czechoslovakia, which provided asylum for persecuted artists (mainly from Nazi Germany), became a space for free creation. If we want to include here at least a brief outline, we have to mention E. F. Burian, creator of the theatre known as D34, and his "light-created scenography" (patented as the Theatregraph by Miroslav Kouřil, 1938). Nor can we speak of Czech set design of the second half of the twentieth century without mentioning František Tröster, who in the thirties moved the development of European set design forward with his construction of dramatic space, working with cubist structures and surrealist visions of new worlds.

However, the thirties were also the years of the painters. They complemented the structure with color, light, and painted shape, close to lyricism. One of them was Jan Sládek, whom we use to demonstrate not only a type of scenery by painters, but also the high standard of the theatre network in the Czech lands at the time (SLADO1–02). Most of his exhibited work from 1931 to 1941 documents the production of the theatre in Ostrava—a mining and industrial city in northern Moravia, in an outlying province, where the composition of the population should indicate weaker cultural needs and traditions. And yet! The theatre here, which was until 1919 German-speaking, energetically and consciously propagated a new linguistic and cultural era in such a way that, as early as the midtwenties, it supported an experimental studio theatre. The majority of professional theatres showed a similarly high cultural level, as did even the amateur groups; as early as the 1920s they worked— often without any time lag—with the latest morphology.

The young Jan Sládek came into the picture at the beginning of the thirties with a generously conceived Shakespearean cycle. The beginning of his career was marked by expressionism and abstractionism. The set for *The Taming of the Shrew* was made up of four colored, movable cubes—the purity of the form has no analogy in Czech set design of those years; experiment here was at the level of creation. Jan Sládek is thus one of the creators of symbolic scenic architecture. He used structured materials capable of catching the light and from the forties worked with drapery as a painterly and spatial element. The motifs of arcades, grills, and graphic articulation, related to a certain phase of Josef Svoboda's postwar work and to some postwar designs by František Tröster, appeared ever more frequently in Sládek's designs.

The efforts made in the first half of the twentieth century to maintain continuity in modern Czech design are summed up in the work of Josef Svoboda. He worked with two of the greatest Czech theatre directors: Alfréd Radok, whom he considers to have been his teacher, and Otomar Krejča, with whom he collaborated in the first real interpretations of Anton Chekhov's plays (SVOB02). He placed his seal on the stage design of our days, furnishing it with expressive means from the field of the fine arts and the fields of optics, acoustics, mechanics, and electronics. Technology is for him a state of mind; it underpins his best work, inspires him, and helps him to realize his ideas, to create what he called a psychoplastic space, capable of sharing in the dramatic action, following it in the different shadings of individual responses, and even substituting for action in moments of poetic silence. Technology thus stands behind his definition of the function of set design; it helps him to rise beyond the light-created theatre of E. F. Burian and Tröster's projects in dramatic space. One of his starting points became the experimental work of the Laterna Magika (Magic Lantern), which at the international exhibition Brussels EXPO 58 made use for the first time of the polyecran technique of multiple projection screens, with Alfréd and Emil Radok as its authors. Svoboda himself used polyecran for the first time on the National Theatre stage in 1959 (Josef Topol's *Their Day*, directed by Otomar Krejča) and again in 1961 in Luigi Nono's opera *Intolleranza* (Teatro La Fenice, Venice, directed by Václav Kašlík).

In the production of *Intolleranza* in Boston (1965, directed by Sarah Caldwell), Svoboda supplemented polyecran with a live film relay from the street and thus made the outside activity a part of the indoor action. He used lasers and holographs in Mozart's *Magic Flute* (Munich 1970, directed by Gunther Rennert), and for Wagner's *Tristan und Isolde* (Wiesbaden 1967, directed by Claus Helmut Drese) he created a tangible and effective cylinder of light from low-volt sources. In the Geneva *Tristan* (1978, SVOB01) he experimented with the director Jean-Claude Riber in creating infinite space and in Richard Strauss's *Die Frau ohne Schatten* (1978) in making shadow a dramatic participant. His expression in set design is always communicated through visual components: painting, color, line, surface, sculptural objects, and the construction of space with a feeling for the synthetic final effect.

At the end of the sixties a weariness with "high style," with ostentatiously composed stage architecture, and with technical effects called forth a reaction: action scenography. The actor became the center of the visual picture, the organizer of the stage, of the meaning and transformations, in an echo of *arte povera*, indicating social and mental deprivation: the humble or destroyed materials of objects on stage, or denim as a material for historical costumes, for example, evoked an interpretation sweeping "grand" drama to the rubbish heap and garbage can.

In the current of this new style of action scenography, Otakar Schindler found himself among set designers younger by more than a generation (SCH101–03). His deliberately eclectic method was in essence a maximally sensitive reaction to the development and specific nature of scenography and fulfilled the declaration of Theo Otto that "if a set designer adheres to a certain style, he becomes a mannerist."

Schindler abandoned the first phase of his work, which emphasized the surrealist visual quality of the surroundings, in favor of the concept of action scenography, which gave preference to the actor as the demiurge of the stage and its transformations. The new poetic led him to the use of natural and authentic materials on the stage, toward the simplification of the concept, toward subdued colors against which the actor stood out. Schindler always devoted his greatest attention to the costume. He liked to work by a collage method in which he combined historical, contemporary, fantastic, and fashionable motifs and used them as character-creating resources. In the eighties, with typical sensitivity toward changes in atmosphere and style, he put into effect a postmodern harmonization of "retro" painted scenery from the nineteenth century, until then generally rejected.

The designer Jaroslav Malina also became a star of action scenography, as a leader among those who formed the new style (MALI01–11). Malina was the pupil of František Tröster, a designer of grand scenic architecture within the proscenium arch; Malina, however, took a different stance. He took his teacher's creation as a challenge when, with a curiosity about space, he extended his interest to the other side of the proscenium arch— to the audience. He stood previous accepted beliefs on their heads and took on the struggle for the cleansing of theatrical media. He preferred natural materials not only because of their authenticity and "reality" but because of their unclichéd emotive effect, and for their new dramatic quality. Drapery was for him a potential space for painting, the bearer of color, softness, changeability. Emotivity and sensuousness—the determining qualities of Malina's signature—were cultivated by experience both from theatre and from painting, for Malina is one of the few to concurrently maintain continuity in his painting. In the depths of his inner experience, in the harmonization of both activities, there is a firm point to which he anchored the area of his work. For *Les Caprices de Marianne* by Alfred de Musset he placed a real tree onstage. Drapery created the space for Shakespeare's *Troilus and Cressida* and Gorki's *Dostigaev and Others*. The colorfulness of the stage for Strindberg's *Miss Julie* is reminiscent of a painted landscape; the lyricism of the scene is broken by the actors in dark costumes as though they had stepped out of a canvas by Edvard Munch (MALI10). Malina's projects reflect developing trends in art; he does not turn his back even on a postmodern point of view. That was demonstrated as early as the eighties; out-of-context Baroque flats form a regular compositional whole for Shakespeare's *Love's Labors Lost* (1987) and *Cymbeline* (1996) and their new "misuse" is part of his reasoning. Even when his essential discoveries are anchored in the set designs, the emphasis on the interpretation of the dramatic hero for more than half the titles is substantiated by the costume.

Miroslav Melena (MELE01–02), who began as an architect, entered action scenography with his regular director and inspirer, Jan Schmid, founder of Studio Ypsilon: "We turned our backs on illusion . . . we put the emphasis on the authenticity and reality of materials" (Jan Schmid). The metamorphic quality of action scenography, the sudden changes of function, the different angles of view on the same phenomenon or object are basic elements of the poetics of the Ypsilon Theatre and of Melena's approach to the reality of the production. In *Macbeth* (1976, directed by Jan Schmid), a set of steps turned into the sides of a festive table, into cliffs with moorland, into the head of Lady Macbeth's bedstead. In the *Play about Mácha* (written and directed by Jan Schmid) the catafalque is a bed, a tower, a range of mountains. In a play about Michelangelo (*Michelangelo Buonarroti*, written and directed by Jan Schmid), the costume and set design were combined: the pope's mantle became a curtain.

Pastel colors, light, and purity of construction characterized Melena's set design up to the 1990s: for Ladislav Klíma's *Matìj Poctivý* (*Matthew the Honest*) the set design is as if made of Lego, easy to take apart, ingenious, clean. Even environments where dilapidation and poverty are directly indicated acquire in Melena's execution the purity and precision of a child's building set.

From the mid seventies the stage design for the Ostrava Petr Bezruč Theatre has been in the hands of Marta Roszkopfová, one of the most distinctive personalities of Czech stage design in the last quarter of the twentieth century (fig. 14, ROSZ06; ROSZ01–05; ROSZ07–08). The combination of Slovak and Polish teaching methods as the two foundation stones of her work provides a partial explanation of the exceptional intensity of her scenic landscapes and costumes. Her immersion in the tasks of production is such that she does not have the need to devote herself to other design activities. For her the dramatic text provides the theme; the director, the idea. Perhaps because she concentrates exclusively on drama, her designs have the hallmark of a ready-made artifact: definitive in the sense of concentrated strength, overflowing from costume design onto stage design, from the environment onto the figure. Even reproductions of her designs betray her overwhelming feeling for color (gray tones in which blood-red pools shine—e.g., in Samuel Beckett's *Endgame*), a feeling for the three-dimensionality of the scenic object (bunkers for *Romeo and Juliet*, ROSZ06), and a grand perception of space (nostalgic backcloths for Eugene O'Neill's *A Moon for the Misbegotten*). Her costumes are shaped in a similarly striking way. She understands the environment and the actor as a dramatic and visual unity. The disassociated quality of the creative team creates an "atmosphere of mutual dependence, loss of concentration, even conflict."

At the 1979 Prague Quadrennial the previously unknown stage designer Jan Vančura won the silver medal for design and costumes for Karel and Josef Čapek's *Insect Play* (F. X. Šalda Theatre, Liberec, directed by Karel Kříž). His exhibited designs did not take into account functionality, which in these years of the flowering of action scenography was a primary requirement. They were difficult to classify—they related most closely to nontheatrical painted works by the artist himself, whose thematic central point is formed by the ornate exteriors and interiors of theatre buildings. And so to him even the environment of the drama is always a sumptuous painting; Vančura's work is decorative in its essence. This was why he was so attracted to the set designs of Karl Friedrich Schinkel, why he turned—the first of us—to the Romantics and to the nineteenth century. However, in spite of this, the sight of the intrusively orange paint which spills over the set for Kopit's *Indians* (fig.

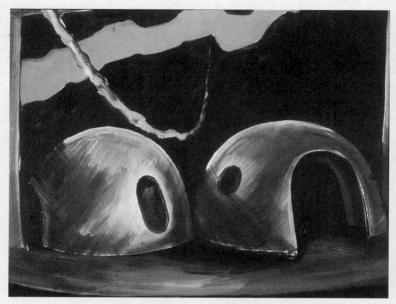

14. ROSZ06. Marta Roszkopfová's "bunker" design for *Romeo and Juliet*, directed by Josef Janík, Petr Bezruč Theatre, 1988.

15. VANC01. Icons of the American West dominate Jan Vančura's design for *Indians*, directed by Petr Palouš, F. X. Šalda Theatre, 1987.

15, VANC01), gets under the skin, underlines the tragedy of events, signals the horror of prepared genocide. Some of his Romantic scenery (for he does use classic painted scenery) seems to be riveted from metal sheets for sci-fi machines; if it tends as a whole toward the past, there are details which place it in our time. The conflict between the needs of former times and the experience of twentieth-century humanity forms one of the magnets of Vančura's artistic work.

For decades costume has remained in the shadow of set design. If, in the first quarter of the twentieth century, set and costumes were artistically unified, in the thirties a rupture occurred which has still not been healed; its result has been the development of the costume designer as a specialist. In the midseventies Josef Jelínek gave costume his primary attention (fig. 16, JELI01; JELI02–03). If his colleagues were expressing color, three-dimensionality, line, and grotesque exaggeration, for Jelínek the prime inspiration was the material itself. He collected and put together authentic embroidery, lace, and textiles (just as the constructivists once discovered natural materials) and from their collage created visually dramatic creations. The complicated composition of these textiles required similarly unusual patterns; experimentation with the technology of fabrics and their sophisticated combination was worked into shapes whose subtle details tend toward a mannerist decorative quality.

The works of both Jana Preková and Simona Rybáková are, through their feeling for the visual and the dramatic, clearly anchored in the late twentieth century. Yet Rybáková's work is extremely extroverted, in the sense of drawing on a range from grand opera to the video clip, while Preková tries to search for hidden connections and to penetrate the depths of dramatic themes. Perhaps with a view to the end of the previous millennium, to the unleashing of the incomprehensible, in both artists one can feel a fascination with death—a fascination which, unlike that of the famous theatrical Poles of the sixties, the directors Jerzy Grotowski and Tadeusz Kantor, does not emphasize destruction, decay, and disintegration, but the millennial possibilities of reincarnation, as in the mummies of the ancient world.

Jana Preková's costumes, which we see here divorced from the action, stimulate the viewer in the same way as a jigsaw puzzle, referring to spheres accessible only to the initiated (fig. 17, PREK01). And onstage they envelop their wearer as an unclear indication; they lure him or her

16. JELI01. Josef Jelínek's distinctive use of textiles is clearly seen in his costume design for the ballet version of *Macbeth*, directed by Antonín Moskalyk, Nová scéna (New Stage) of the National Theatre, 1984.

17. PREKO1. Jana Preková was awarded a gold medal for this installation of her costume designs at the Prague Quadrennial, 1999.

into a trap by the tightness of their fit, the length of their sleeves. The execution is stirring, for "the spirit is awakened when both beauty and ugliness are present," says the designer. Her stage composition also splinters into drama: as after an explosion, hermetic symbols are scattered around the stage like charges. A continuation of Czech spatial paths in the direction of deconstruction? Preková however calls the

18. STEZ02. Zuzana Štefunková costume design for *Werther*, directed by Peter Gábor, Middle Bohemian Theatre, 1997.

environment that her dramatic heroes enter "an experimental silence, a white desolation an experiment in emptiness." So it seems that today many set designers approach "the minimalist form . . . a blank sheet of paper," and Jana Preková too approaches this method of thought in much of her work.

19. RYBA01. Simona Rybáková's postmodern mannerism resulted in
the use of plastic fruit in her costumes for *Piece by Piece*, directed
by Michal and Šimon Caban, Czech Television, 1998.

After the constructivist space of Hofman, the hyperbole of Tröster,
and the "psychoplasticism" of Svoboda, at the end of the eighties a space
was provided for the play which was more sensitive and personal, similar to that described by Peter Scherhaufer, the renowned dramaturg and
director of the Goose on a String Theatre in Brno, in his book *Inscenace
v nepravidelném prostoru* (*Production in An Irregular Space*, 1989). The
best creations of Zuzana Štefunková belong to a similar spatial silence
(fig. 18, STEZ02). Her good fortune at the beginning of her career in finding excellent directors and production teams has enabled her to find her
own style and opinion very quickly.

The fantastic creations of Simona Rybáková "swallow" the space (fig.
19, RYBA01). The costumes provoke with their strikingly surprising materials—plastic products, graters, nails—things which above all ironize
contemporary consumer society. With the set designer Daniel Dvořák,

Rybáková put her name to a cycle of Mozart operas, performed beginning in 1992 in summer seasons at the Theatre of the Estates in Prague. The sense and the point of the situations flow without previously given rules; it is "reckless treatment of the ruins of the past, the rococo of the nineties." Her costumes come close to sculpture; with perverse focus Rybáková loads on them towering wigs, plastic scrolled sleeves, bizarre hats, wicker baskets with fruit, and so on. Deformation of the body with the help of padding changes the actor into an artifact.

The circle is closed: we began with Arcimboldo's work and found an Arcimboldo for the end of the millennium. Here we close with the merry mannerism inspired by his creation.

Note: The quotes throughout this chapter are from conversations the author has had with the various set designers.

■ ■ ■

DENNIS P. CHRISTILLES

Czech Scenography in America

■ ■ ■

If asked why an exhibition of Czech scenography is of interest to theatre practitioners and audiences in the United States, one might reply that it invites a reexamination of our own theatrical art. A place where we rediscover ourselves, the theatre is a sacred space where we are "made strange"—looked at through a sideward glance—in order to more clearly see our humanity. The works in this exhibit make strange our view of our own theatre and lead us to a richer understanding of who we are and who we might become. What we see hanging on these walls should not surprise us. It will instead serve as a reaffirmation for us. These artists have traveled many of the same roads that American theatre artists have traveled; they were often down those roads before anyone else. The works that make up this exhibition are a reflection not only of the rich theatrical tradition of the Czech Republic, but a mirror of the best of our own theatre here in the United States. Many of the precepts of Czech design are precepts that we have long ago embraced and made our own. We have often done this without realizing where the idea may have come from or how it came to us—perhaps as only a flash of an image or a whisper of an idea—a part of the aesthetic atmosphere.

Czech scenography has its roots in a number of rich and varied soils. Important movements in the visual arts such as symbolism, cubism, expressionism, and surrealism have all served to lend inspiration. The linguistic theories of the Prague structuralists of the 1930s and early 1940s added a solid theoretical foundation. Semiotics is alive with the exploration and search for meaning and meanings in theatre and film. Reading the works of the early theorists of the Prague school, one finds their words made manifest by the designers presented in the exhibit.

Many of these theorists (Otakar Zich, Jan Mukařovsky, Petr Bogatyrev, Jiří Veltruský, and Jindřich Honzl) may be seen as proponents of principles that describe the work of Czech scenographic artists. In some ways these ideas defined and liberated scenographic art. A fundamental principle of semiotic theatrical study is that everything that is placed on stage serves as an intentional sign—a communicator of meaning. This means that decoration for its own sake is out, and carefully devised environments and costumes are essential. While it is probable that pioneer Czech scenographers may not have viewed semiotic theory as injunctive, it is very easy to conclude through an examination of their writings that the early semiotic theorists of Prague influenced theatrical practice of their day. It is credible to suppose that these ideas were a part of the artistic and intellectual milieu of Prague in the 1930s and 1940s. This connection has been well established by many observers such as the contemporary Slovak theatre theoretician Ladislav Lajcha.

It is basic to theatre to say that it is an operation of the imagination. Semioticians speak of the transformability of a sign. That is, its meaning changes according to how it is viewed or how it is used. In the theatre a chair might represent a whole class of chairs or, through suggestion, something else altogether. If the chair is used as a throne, even the simplest of wooden constructions becomes, for that instant, a regal seat. In the next instant it might be called upon to be a cloud, a mountain, or a pile of trash. In the theatre this can happen!

Czech stage designers long ago recognized and embraced this fundamental aspect of theatrical performance and metaphorically went to town with it. The Czech stage is a fertile field of imaginative spinning, dancing, ever-changing images that complement and contradict one another, creating meaning and questions.

What we see hanging on the walls of this exhibit are the springboards of these imaginative explorations. They are, in some ways, only the relics of that which can never be accurately recorded—that is, the unstoppable movement through time of the theatrical performance. It has never truly been captured on film or video tape, for it is a thing that can only exist in time before a live audience.

But these relics, these springboards are far from silent. They sing with excitement, with inventive line and color. These compositions stand apart from the performances in which they were once participants. They are art unto themselves. They are a collection of individual styles and personalities.

Looking at the works, one can delight in the painterly poetry of Jaroslav Malina (MALI11) and the architectural lyricism of Josef Svoboda (SVOBO1). The exciting individual styles of Jan Vančura (VANC02) and Otakar Schindler (SCHI01) distinguish them as outstanding painters. The works in this exhibition are a part of and yet transcend the theatre.

One of the most important aspects of this exhibit of scenography is that it represents a kind of theatre that is essential. It represents theatre operating as an instrument of truth. Many of the productions represented here were accomplished during times of repression and censorship. Under Nazism and under communism the truth was a rare commodity—and a dangerous one. Because of the elusive nature of theatre and the highly metaphorical means employed by its practitioners, the theatre was an arena in which the truth might be heard. Joy and suffering alike might be shared in a circumspect way in a public place. Official censors had a difficult if not impossible task in defining the precise meaning of suspect metaphors that never seemed to sit still to have their meanings "photographed" for the official records.

So Czech theatre design represents a theatre that is an active agent in society; ironically public and yet secret—a shared secret between audience and theatre artists. It was often through the transformability of the visual signs onstage that a truer understanding of society was communicated. The dramatic text of the playwright, often seemingly innocent in regard to political content, was only a single channel of communication. The physical and psychological use of the actor's body and costume in relationship to the stage space created a subtext of meaning. This subtext (the physical spectacle of the theatre design) most often spoke quite eloquently in the secret language of irony and metaphor.

Czech stage design of the twentieth century has always placed the scenographer as an equal partner within the hierarchy of theatre artists. These artists have explored through visual means the deeper truths that are the aims of the dramatic text and often what lies beyond it. In a sense it is the scenographic environment itself that takes the stage as another actor. This actor is seldom silent and is forever alive. This other actor is the subtext, or several subtexts, of the theatre performance; it is the secret sharer of all that is seen and unseen, spoken and unspoken. This highly metaphorical approach to theatre capitalizes on what theatre does best. Theatre is at its best when it suggests rather than explicates, reveals rather than explains, and inspires rather than dictates. Czech stage design and Czech theatre in general are theatre at its best.

In this respect the Czech theatre lives as model for theatres of all nations to emulate. The works in this exhibition offer powerful testament to this living legacy.

■ ■ ■

DELBERT UNRUH

Modernism to Imagism

■ ■ ■

Metaphor and Irony 2, when coupled with its predecessor, Metaphor and Irony, provided a complete view of Czech theatre design. Beginning with the work of František Tröster in 1936 and ending with productions completed as recently as 2003, this exhibit encompassed the visual art of the Czech theatre from modernism to imagism.

These sixty-seven years were a remarkable time in the theatre in the Czech Republic—a time of great contrasts and ironies—a phrase that encapsulates the history of this vibrant and creative people, from the World War I armistice that created the modern state of Czechoslovakia out of the rubble of the Austro-Hungarian empire; to its imprisonment—first under the Nazis in 1938 and later behind the Iron Curtain in 1945; to the Velvet Revolution of 1989; to the split of the country into the two independent states of Slovakia and the Czech Republic in 1993; to the referendum in June of 2003 affirming the desire of the citizens of the Czech Republic to join the European Union; and finally, to membership in the EU on 1 May 2004.

A turbulent history, survived always by the unique Czech national consciousness composed equally of the grotesque and the ridiculous, Franz Kafka and Soldier Schweik, metaphor and irony. And it is in the theatre that this consciousness is most evident, for theatre has always been at the center of Czech life. It was the Czech citizens who donated the money to build the first National Theatre in Prague in 1881 and then again in 1883 after the first building burned. It was in the theatres that Czechs could hear the truth spoken during the time of the socialist repression. It was the theatre students who were at the forefront of the early demonstrations of the Velvet Revolution. It was in the theatres that the pivotal meetings of Civic Forum were held, and it was Václav Havel, a playwright, who was elected as president of the new Czech Republic. These exhibitions provided us with insight into the major artistic movements—modernism, scenography, action design, and imagism—that have shaped this theatre.

Beginning with the early work of František Tröster (TROS01–13), in the thirties and forties modernism, particularly cubism and surrealism, entered into contemporary Czech theatre design. Tröster's work established the basis for contemporary Czech stage design, and his influence is still felt today (in many ways Tröster is the equivalent of Robert Edmond Jones in the United States). Sadly, the decade from approximately 1945 to 1955 was a dark one for Tröster and the Czech theatre as the communists harshly imposed the principles of socialist realism—an artistic theory which officially denounced any production techniques that were not naturalistic or socially optimistic.

However, following the official denunciation of Stalin by Khrushchev at the Twentieth Party Congress in 1956, a new style of visual thinking became possible, and the pressure that had built up for ten years in the artistic community burst out into a new creative flowering characterized by an abstract, kinetic, and metaphoric style of stage design known as scenography. Originally developed by Tröster as an expansion of modernism, scenography incorporated the latest technological advances into stage design. This nonliteral and evocative approach to stage design and production became almost a secret language that challenged audiences to see expanded possibilities in life beyond simple creature comforts. The ideas and techniques of scenography were augmented, expanded, and popularized worldwide by Josef Svoboda (SVOB01–02) and Ladislav Vychodil at the National Theatre complexes in Prague and Bratislava, respectively. Theatrical design and production reached a high artistic level, and from 1958 to 1963 the work of Tröster, Svoboda, and Vychodil garnered the highest awards in international competitions in Brussels and São Paulo.

But these new creative impulses were not strong enough to withstand the brutal crushing of the Dubček government and the Prague Spring in August 1968 by the armies of the Warsaw Pact. The reimposition of hardline communist rule threatened to stamp out all the artistic gains that had been achieved, and cultural restrictions again became strict and severe. Four factors, however, made it possible for some of the creative freedoms to be preserved in the theatre.

First, the cultural authorities focused most of their energy on reimposing cultural restrictions on radio, television, and print publication.

Theatre was censored, to be sure, but established scripts and the classics could always be approved for production. In reality, many productions of these scripts were structured by the artists and viewed by the audience as subtle protests against the status quo. Second, the large state-supported National Theatre complexes in Prague and Bratislava, viewed as official cultural monuments by the authorities, came under the closest scrutiny and had the tightest controls reimposed. Third, the smaller experimental theatres, while still under state control and subsidy, were allowed to continue. Their work was officially tolerated, and artists learned over time how they could communicate the truth to their audiences through abstract, sly, nonverbal, and metaphoric means. These theatres attracted the best directors, designers, and actors of the new generation and were the source of bold theatrical experiments. Fourth, the ability to do this kind of work in the avant-garde theatres was made possible by the fact that the reimposition of strict cultural restrictions did not reimpose the rules of socialist realism on theatre design.

Ironically, the period of "normalization" that was supposed to stamp out all revolutionary activity in the country after 1968 inadvertently sowed the seeds of one of the most remarkable revolutions in theatre production and design. The secret language hinted at in the scenographic style began to transform itself in the experimental theatres throughout the country into a complex theatrical grammar that allowed theatre artists, in silent agreement with their audiences, to talk truthfully about present-day life in their country. Led by the bold departures of Jaroslav Malina (fig. 20, MALI11; MALI01–10), this new generation of designers, including Helena Anýžová (ANYZ01–05), Jan Dušek (DUSE01–10), Petr Matásek (fig. 21, MATA06; MATA01–05, MATA07–12), Marie Franková (fig. 22, FRAN04; FRAN01–03; FRAN05), Marta Roszkopfová (ROSZ01–08), and Ivo Židek (ZIDE01–03), and later Jana Zbořilová (fig. 23, ZBOR02; ZBOR01, ZBOR03–05), Karel Glogr (fig. 24, GLOG04; GLOG01–03), and Dana Hávová (HAVO01–10), developed and refined a new style of theatrical design. Known as action design, it became the visual partner of the best productions in the Czech theatres from approximately 1965 to 1990. Action design existed on two levels simultaneously. On the surface it was simple, functional, abstract, and seemingly disconnected from the present-day reality of life in Czechoslovakia. But below the surface existed a complex web of metaphorical associations and ironic references that audiences understood and responded to as mirrors of their present-day

20. MALI11. Jaroslav Malina envisions the American South through the prism of his action design for *The Ballad of the Sad Cafe*, directed by Jiří Fréhar, E. F. Burian Theatre, 1987.

concerns. Three production ideas—author's theatre, universal space, and open communication—were the bases of action design.

In author's theatre the designer, director, and company of performers built up a performance through discussion, improvisation, and group collaboration that would result in a complete performance scenario written down later by a dramaturg. This method of production, made possible by state support, extended rehearsal schedules and supported a company concept that made long-term collaborative relationships possible. This process became so popular that its techniques were used as a model by the directors, designers, and actors working with established scripts.

The idea of universal space was inclusive and functional, not closed and descriptive. This theatrical space provided the requisites for the dramatic and physical action for the performer and spoke on an aesthetic plane to the audience by evoking specific emotions, while simultaneously drawing both performer and audience member into the same physical space. This space, the artists believed, made open communication between audience and stage possible.

Open communication meant that the exchange between the stage and the audience would be honest and direct and would not place any philo-

21. MATA06. Petr Matásek's puppet, Naděžda, used in *Cirkus Unikum*, directed by Josef Krofta, Drak Theatre, 1978. Photo by Joe Brandesky.

sophical or aesthetic barriers between the production and the audience. Socially, the idea meant a tacit agreement on the part of artists and audiences that moral issues would be discussed as openly as the political situation would permit. In many ways the theatre of this time functioned as a weapon against the totalitarian regime, and the result was that the truth was spoken, continuously, for thirty years in the Czech theatre.

And the truth spoken in these theatres, along with other social pressures, finally brought down the socialists. Out of the ensuing upheaval

22. FRAN04. Marie Franková's distinctive watercolor design for *The Inspector General*, directed by Ivan Balad'a, Municipal Theatre in Zlín, 1999.

the principles of action design were more or less discarded. They were seen as being too identified with previous opposition to the socialist regime. A new, eclectic, imagistic style of design, which borrows from any source—television, motion pictures, performance art, installation art, period decoration, kitsch, trash cans, advertising, the Internet—has emerged in the Czech theatre. This style, most closely identified with the

23. ZBOR02. Jana Zbořilová's mask and costume for *The Firebird*, directed by Zbyněk Srba, Theatre of the Estates, 2000.

work of the new generation—David Marek (fig. 25, MARE01; MARE02–04), Sylva Zimula Hanáková (fig. 26, ZIMU02; ZIMU01, ZIMU03–04), Jan Štěpánek (fig. 27, STEP02; STEP01, STEP03–06), Petra Štětinová Goldflamová (STET01–06), Egon Tobiáš (fig. 28, TOBI04; TOBI01–03), Kateřina Štefková (fig. 29, STEF01; STEF02–07)—has been

24. GLOG04. Karel Glogr's setting for *August, August, August*, directed by Karel Nováček, Stibor Theatre in Olomouc, 1990.

adopted in subtle ways by the previous generation of designers as they too adjust to the new realities of life and art in a media-driven market economy. In its most extreme form, imagism is almost the visual antithesis of all that came before. Forsaking allusion, metaphor, and, sometimes, logical narrative, the artists working in image theatre (an idea also evolving in our own theatre) seek to create a dynamic space that fires a series of visual shocks at the audience. This style of design, the artists maintain, is more in tune with the postmodern era of the present day.

However, no matter what stylistic name observers like me have pinned on it throughout time, Czech stage design has always adapted and changed with the new realities of life in the nation. The images in this book are a record of that change. The best theatre design, in any time and culture, is a reflection of the social and political dynamics that surround it, and the best theatrical designers are astute observers of, and adapt to, the time and culture they live in. In a conversation with Jaroslav Malina in 2000 I asked him how his philosophy of design had

25. MARE01. David Marek's design for *The Artless*,
directed by Michal Dočekal, Tyl Theatre, 2001.

changed over the years. Malina was a student of Tröster, a leader in the formation of the aesthetic of action design, a teacher of the newest generation, and an internationally respected contemporary designer. He responded immediately: "I believe now that stage design must have fitness for purpose." Fitness for purpose—speak to your audience—a sophisticated philosophy and view of stage design that has always characterized the ever-evolving work of the remarkable designers featured in the Metaphor and Irony exhibit.

26. ZIMU02. An all-male cast wore Sylva Zimula Hanáková costumes for *Richard III*, directed by Vladimir Morávek, Theatre Globe, 2001. Photo by Viktor Kronbauer.

27. STEP02. Jan Štěpánek's free rendering style is evident in this design for *Šarka*, directed by Jiří Pokorný, Tyl Theatre, 2000.

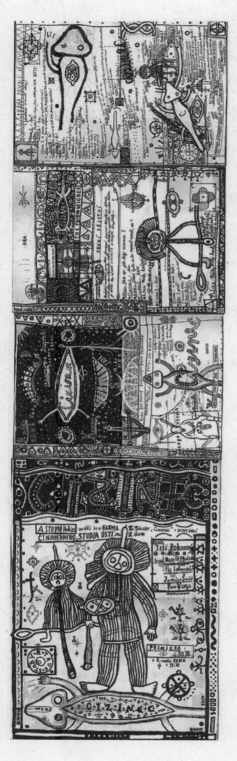

28. TOB104. The imagistic trend in Czech design as seen in Egon Tobiáš's poster for his production of *The Foreigner*, Drama Studio in Ústí nad Labem, 1994.

29. STEF01. Kateřina Štefková's lush costume designs for *Fernando Krapp Wrote Me a Letter*, directed by Petr Lébl, Theatre Labyrint, 1992.

■ ■ ■

MARIE ZDEŇKOVÁ

Authority, Playfulness, Metaphor, and Irony

■ ■ ■

It is appropriate that this essay on modern Czech stage design begins with František Tröster, whose centenary was celebrated in 2004. Both early and later developments of modern Czech stage design meet in Tröster's work.

František Tröster, architect and urban planner, entered the world of professional theatre at the beginning of the 1930s, a time when various currents encountered each other and interchanged on the artistic scene in Czechoslovakia. He experienced expressionism in the theatre (the dramatized use of angular cubist morphology); a movement established on the Prague stage by the architect Vlastislav Hofman. He absorbed the influences of French surrealism and Russian constructivism, established by young adherents of the interwar avant-garde who from the 1920s founded small, experimental studio theatres. "The new synthetic theatre, enriched by the cubist discovery of structure and the Surrealist discovery, not in any way of new ornaments but of new worlds, strives not only for the dream, but for its confrontation with reality."[1] An interest in collage and film (editing, montage, rhythm, enlargement) was something else that linked Tröster with the avant-garde.

The short period he spent as an urban planner also helped to equip him. In Algiers he dealt with the planning of a difficult, undulating terrain. He consciously made use of this experience in his stage design. "Urban planning also has to define space. It has to give order to wild terrain. Of course, not against its nature."[2] Tröster liked Italian towns, soaked in culture. He found their visual aspect dramatic. Later he appreciated sculptural architecture, in whose spirit Oscar Niemeyer built the new city of Brasilia at the turn of the 1950s and 1960s. In spite of his knowledge of so many artistic styles Tröster committed himself to none of them, and everything he learned from the "isms" he put to the service of dramatic function. His predecessor Vlastislav Hofman likewise gave preference to the dramatic function of stage design. The expressionist style, in itself dramatic, was subordinated to the theatrical effect. He made use of it in scene painting and architecture. Tröster went further. He was fascinated by the phenomenon of space. "The basis of stage action is space. The stage itself is a hollow cube, into which an artificial, dramatic space has to be inserted."[3] He approached dramatic space as someone with the authority of a scholar and explorer would approach the universe and nature, subordinate to physical laws. The world of theatrical work was for him linked with reality, but at the same time he acknowledged its specific exclusivity: "From actual elements we composed a new reality which could exist only on stage and only on stage could be truthful. . . . Illusion is in essence a slice of chaos without concentration and composition—the conscious choice of things, how they are put together and linked, is the basis of art."[4]

Tröster worked also with other nonmaterial elements of stage design such as movement, time, rhythm, and light. He conceived light not in any way as a mood-maker, but chiefly as an element-shaping material on the surface of the set and on the architectural forms of the stage. The ground plan of the acting space was made rhythmical by a system of angled lines and backcloths. He determined the space of the stage by a composition of three-dimensional objects, varying in confrontation with the actor's movement. He felt not only architecturally but sculpturally.

"First," he said, "it is necessary for the director and the designer to find a shared attitude towards the subject. Another approach resembles sculptural work. The weight of the play is laid bare up to certain firm points which create the future skeleton of the dramatic creation."[5] This comparison is something of a metaphor, but it applies both vicariously and to concrete work. Tröster worked on Shakespeare's *Julius Caesar* (National Theatre, Prague, 1936) with the director Jiří Frejka, originally an initiator of the small avant-garde theatre of the 1920s. The larger-than-life sculptures (a bust of the emperor and the lower fragment of an equestrian statue, one horse's hoof stepping forward) were installed on a massive inclined plinth and in that way were presented like photo shots from a worm's-eye view (the influence of Soviet film montage). Through this the scenic elements gained strength and, as it were, spatially crushed the figures of the actors, which seemed diminished and somehow petty in contrast (Tröster did not consider this to be a symbol, but an "opinion"). The visual angle of the audience's view was likewise adjusted by three rotating slopes on the front of the stage, which made it possible for the performers' actions to be viewed from above and below. Such a dramatizing deformation of reality is comparable to expressionist abbreviation. "By contrast with [expressionism] we changed the direction of expression. We transferred its vanishing point to the auditorium."[6]

Another famous production in which Frejka and Tröster shaped space and made it more dynamic was Gogol's *Government Inspector* (National Theatre, Prague, 1936). The drunken Khlestakov makes his entrance along an angled walkway from the depths of the stage and—in rhythm with his drunken gait—expressively inclined doors descend in front of him from the grid. The dance of the doors ends at the moment when a platform with a couch rises from the orchestra pit and Khlestakov throws himself on it. The space plays and changes in parallel with the performer's action and in that sense is a dynamic action space.

The fundamental starting point of the time/space program of the production was the collaborative directing and design "re-reading" of the subject of the play. Tröster considered the director to be the creator and guarantor of the stage interpretation of the drama. The actor was the main user and measure of the functionality of the stage, and should not be overshadowed by its expansion.

After World War II a large part of Tröster's creative activity was concentrated on the educational field. In 1946 he played a role in the founding of the department of stage design in the Theatre Faculty of the Academy of Performing Arts in Prague (DAMU). He was interested in young talent and the development of contemporary theatre. There were however certain aspects with which he was not satisfied. Although before the war he himself dreamed of developing the technical possibilities of stage design, he was a sharp critic of the expansion of technique in some contemporary productions (still famous today), blaming them for subordinating the acting element to attractive scenographic eclecticism. He distanced himself from the work of Josef Svoboda, who in a technically perfected form continued with his "psychoplastic" space based on Tröster's work. He saw hope for renewal of the theatre in young designers.

Although Tröster himself worked in large theatres all his life (the National Theatre in Prague, the Regional Theatre in Brno), it was the small theatres founded on the affinity of a creative team, which fulfilled his idea of creative workshops. In the 1960s he welcomed the growing spectrum of small stages, and wrote of the need to maintain the independence of individual small theatres: he named specifically the

Divadlo Na zábradlí (Theatre on the Balustrade), Činoherní klub (Drama Club), and Studio Y in Liberec. Originality was for him the highest of all values. He conceived it not only as an artistic value but also as a mark of personal integrity. His instruction was intensive and non-traditional. "He would give a lecture which started out from a very simple impulse which he then developed and compared with his own experience. It was a concentrate of everything embracing art, philosophy and aesthetics."[7]

As a charismatic and problematic personality, Tröster was for students both a scourge and an admired teacher. His requirements of authority and consistency in their work were conveyed in an attractive way. "Tröster knew how to motivate and engage his students. . . . When for example he [discussed] Carmen, he sang, slunk along the wall and played a smuggler."[8] Although no Tröster clones emerged from DAMU, his influence as a teacher was incontestable. The discovery of the special dynamic qualities of the stage space, the accentuation of the dramatic function of stage design, and the need for teamwork were handed on by his pupils to their pupils in the same department (Jan Dušek, Jaroslav Malina, Albert Pražák, Marie Franková).

What became known as action scenography began to be implemented in Czechoslovakia at the turn of the 1960s and 1970s. It was Tröster's pupils who were the main bearers of this trend (Malina, Dušek, Miroslav Melena). Their method of work was distinct from the architectural and painted stage design of the time (Oldřich Šimáček, Zbyněk Kolář, Květoslav Bubeník), in which the artists made use of the effectiveness of architectural forms and metaphors of visual detail and laid their compositions before the audience like a stage picture framed by the proscenium arch.

The artist and stage designer Libor Fára is considered a pioneer of action scenography. In Alfred Jarry's Ubu roi (Divadlo Na zábradlí, 1964) he made garbage cans and a collapsible brass bed "perform." As the collective idea of a generation, action scenography was born and grew up in theatres outside Prague, on small, studio-type stages: in Brno, the Divadlo Husa na provázku (Goose on a String Theatre), founded in 1968, and the HaDivadlo (HaTheatre), 1974; in Ústí nad Labem, the Činoherní studio (Drama Studio), 1972; in Liberec, the Studio Y, 1963; and even on the larger stages of the more "official" municipal theatres: the Divadlo F. X. Šalda in Liberec; the Divadlo Petra Bezruče in Ostrava; the Divadlo pracujících (Workers' Theatre) in Gottwaldov, now Zlín. Like-minded creative teams originated in these places, among them designer Jaroslav Malina and director Karel Kříž; designer Miroslav Melena and director Jan Schmid; designer Marta Roszkopfová and director Josef Janík; designer Ivo Žídek and director Ivan Rajmont, and so on.

At the turn of the 1970s and 1980s, when President Husák's "normalization" began to relax just a little, action scenography began to reach Prague. In 1978 Studio Y from Liberec, led by designer-director Jan Schmid, moved to Prague in its entirety. During the 1980s individuals worked as guest directors and designers in the small theatres. Some of them even broke through to the stage of the National Theatre, among them Jaroslav Malina, Marie Franková, and Jan Dušek.

The young designers of the action scenography movement had no ambitions (and usually no opportunities or means) to model the stage architecturally or sculpturally. Their starting point was Tröster's legacy: the stage is the actor's territory and its changeability is closely linked with the dramatic action (fig. 30, TROS13; TROS01–12). However, the author of the scenic element is not the stage technician, but the actor himself. The action of the performer has as its result the movement of the scene—its change. This change is not only an indication of a change in place but also relates to the meaning, and even has an emotional impact. The manipulation of an object (part of the set) thus creates a stage metaphor and the atmosphere of a particular situation. Most suitable for action scenography are simple, easily manipulated objects (rope, boxes, drapery), but the design could include the "more difficult" garbage can or barrel. Suspended ropes could be a forest; knotted together, the trunk of a single tree, a net, or a gallows (Jan Dušek). Drapery could represent the sails of a ship, a tent, the foliage of a tree, or the sky (Jaroslav Malina). Living scenery, scenery in movement, scenery in the hands of the actor was open to chance and improvisation.

Otherwise ordinary materials discovered on rubbish heaps or in junk shops, were used as much for their practical qualities as for their capacity to support aesthetic rationales and period feel. Decoration was foreign to the designers of this generation; they were attracted to the exploration of the qualities of various materials and their direct effect. That connected them to the European experimental theatres of the time and the visual arts generally—the anti-decorative and, at the same time, visual and emotional "poor theatre," "aesthetic ugliness," finding aesthetic qualities in corrosion, in destroyed and thrown-out objects, for

30. TROS13. František Tröster's sculptural setting for *The Winter's Tale*, directed by Jaromír Pleskot, National Theatre, 1965.

example. However, Czech artists for the most part adapted accepted trends to their own needs. They lightened the rawness and commented with humor—their playfulness was inherited from the interwar avant-garde, which understood the stage as a space for provocatively triggered play, they upset austerity and asceticism (often ironically) by use of decorative details. Under a totalitarian regime, "metaphor and irony" became weapons and, by conspiratorial method, a means of communication with an audience which came to the theatre to taste at least the atmosphere of freedom.

Further aspects of this trend were explored through the use of nontraditional space. If designers were working in a traditional proscenium-arch theatre, they tried to take the play into spaces other than the stage itself (the foyer, the front of the theatre, etc.) or to furnish the auditorium with atypical scenic elements, such as drapery overarching the stage or trunks of trees in both the stage and the auditorium.

Costume, stylized expressively and daringly, was an important element of the production. Its metaphorical communicability, underpinned by stylistic quotation, was often heterogeneous to the point of an absurd combination of various historical elements. This occurred almost twenty years before the impact of postmodernism was felt in Bohemia. The concept and appearance of the set and costumes were closely connected, whether in the sense of stylistic unity or contrast. It was not unusual for the set and costumes to be designed by the same designer, a link to the past practices of Vlastislav Hofman.

The end of the 1980s brought a continual oscillation between functionality and visual quality that issued in a tide of postmodernism. The structured and boundless quotation of various styles was divided into operetta/musical decoration (sometimes seasoned with irony) and a concentrated synthesis in intellectually ambitious projects, first at the small and later the official theatres. There was a return to visually effective theatre. The picture appeared on the stage again, but this time a three-dimensional, variable picture, not unconnected with the Baroque theatre of scenic attraction. New teams were formed, new relationships developed between directors and designers. The most important directors who were establishing themselves in the 1990s displayed an expressive pictorial vision and became in essence the main guarantors of the visual appearance of the production. Petr Lébl (director and set designer) with Kateřina Štefková, Jan Nebeský with Jana Preková, Michal Dočekal with David Marek, J. A. Pitínský with Tomáš Rusín, Zuzana Štefunková and Jan Štěpánek, Vladimír Morávek with Martin Chocholoušek and Sylva Zimula Hanáková—these teams designed specific worlds full of fantasy and symbols. Some set designers of the preceding generation reevaluated their approaches and graciously accepted the effectiveness, beauty, and attraction of the newer practices. It was not even so much a question of subordination to a period trend as one of concurrent individual development, since the changes in these artists' work began to appear even before the onset of postmodernism and the theatre of scenic pictures.

After the Velvet Revolution nonconformist artists had the opportunity to work on the official stages. In the same way as the interwar avant-garde, they gained experience on both small and large stages. Small theatres obviously did not disappear and continued to attract creative and searching designers. A number of new little theatres came into existence: in Prague the Spolek Kašpar (Kašpar Company), Divadlo v

Dlouhé (Theatre in Dlouhá Street), Pražské komorní divadlo (Prague Chamber Theatre), as a rule bringing together the younger generation of artists.

At the present time it seems that the starting point for the designer-director is not the action, but rather the visual expression of the world of the play, of the situation, of the dramatic character. Tröster's vision is still valid, although on other principles and in another form: the set creates the cosmos of the drama.

NOTES

1. Vladislav Stanovský, "Divadlo, škola, města: Hovořime s Františkem Tröstrem" (Theatre, School, City: A Conversation with František Tröster), *Kulturni tvorba* (*Cultural Creation*) 1, no. 7, 1963, in *Scénografie*, Divadelní ústav, Praha 1982, no. 47.

2. František Tröster, "Poznámky o scéně," in Stanovský, "Divadlo."

3. František Tröster, quoted in Vladimír Jindra, "Měřeno dneškem" (Measured by Today), *Divadlo* (*Theatre*) 15, no. 10, 1964, in *Scénografie*, Divadelní ústav, Praha 1982, no. 47.

4. Tröster, "Poznámky o scéně."

5. Tröster, quoted in Jindra, "Měřeno dneškem."

6. Magda Svobodová, *František Tröster a jeho okrul: Scénografie v kontextu české kultury* (*František Tröster and His Circle: Stage Design in the Context of Czech Culture*), doctoral diss., UK FF (Arts Faculty of Charles University), 2002.

7. Svobodová, "František Tröster."

8. Svobodová, "František Tröster."

■ ■ ■

HELENA ALBERTOVÁ & JOSEPH BRANDESKY

Biographies of Designers

■ ■ ■

HELENA ANÝŽOVÁ

Helena Anýžová, costume designer, was born in Pilsen in 1936. She has also worked in film and occasionally as a stage actor. She shared in the work of production teams that implemented action scenography processes in the 1970s and 1980s. Even if this trend pointed toward a striking—even dominant—role for costume in the appearance of a production, the concepts of Anýžová's costumes (including the design drawings) always had a light and subtle effect, with a slight whiff of sensuality. The designer respected the figure of the actor and, for the most part, retained natural proportions, adjusting them only slightly by the arrangement of fabric, detail, and accessories. A simple charm, a subtle humor, and a playful comedy were expressed through her understated, stylized interventions. Her work with the set designer Jaroslav Malina was important for her vision of the production as a whole, since he laid emphasis on the contrasting and harmonic interdependence of set and costume.

Although the means of expression of her personal style did not change in its essentials, she expanded and relaxed their range with the tide of postmodernism. The designs for Mozart's opera *Bastien et Bastienne* (1999), full of casual coquetry, possessed a lightly veiled eroticism and, above all, a subtle but sophisticated humor and irony. For Emil František Burian's *Paříž hraje prim* (*Paris Plays First Fiddle*, 2002), which used a ballad by Francois Villon, Anýžová created costumes which in some cases forsook the modesty of a sensual suggestion and ventured into erotic literalness. A graceful Gothic line echoes in the drawing of figures with a hint of movement and in the more robust stylization of the masqueraders "decorated" with phallic symbols. However, she also implemented a sprightly, quackish, histrionic quality, which suitably warmed up the stone environment of the Gothic castle of Hukvaldy, where the production took place.

JAN DUŠEK

Jan Dušek, designer of sets and costumes, was born in Prague in 1942. From 1962 to 1967 he studied set design with František Tröster in the Theatre Faculty of the Academy of Performing Arts in Prague. In 1977 he became a teacher there and from 1991 has been head of the department of stage design. As a representative of action scenography in the 1970s and 1980s he worked with authentic materials and ordinary objects (doors, boxes, rope, paper) which he composed into situation scenarios relying on the action and performers. He varied an anti-illusionist concept of theatre, connected to Tröster's dynamized performance space, with austere economy and a critically humorous and unsugary playfulness that relied on an element of improvisation.

In the 1990s the range of his means of expression expanded, in connection with contemporary postmodern influences. His set designs for *Příliš hlučná samota* (*Too Loud a Solitude*), based on the 1976 novel by Bohumil Hrabal and dramatized by Evald Schorm, in 1988, is related by the simple spatial organization of ordinary objects to action scenography. His set for Shakespeare's *Othello*, which won the Alfréd Radok Award in 1996, is resolved architecturally; the rhythm of its geometrical shapes recalls the clean forms of the Swiss theatre reformer Adolph Appia and some of those of Josef Svoboda. His designs for Miloš Štědroň's musical based on Romain Rolland's *Le Jeu de l'amour et de la mort* (1998) use a folk element typical for Dušek. The grouping of the ghostly figures into a *mise-en-scène* in confrontation with the scanty but significant furnishings of the set (a guillotine like an isolated Maypole, decapitated heads as scattered heads of cabbage) anticipates in expressive abbreviation the dramatic charge of the production. *The Magic Mountain*, based on the novel by Thomas Mann and dramatized by Štěpán Otčenášek in 1997, became a challenge for Dušek, as co-creator of a visually conceived world for the production by Jan Antonín Pitínský. The designer balanced the ebullient mixture of postmodern visual means used by Pitínský with a rather starkly painted silhouette of alpine peaks.

MARIE FRANKOVÁ

Marie Franková, costume designer, was born in Kopidlna in 1944. From 1961 to 1977 she studied stage design with František Tröster at the Theatre Faculty of the Academy of Performing Arts in Prague, where she later taught costume design (1990–2000). At present she also works for television and film. Her cooperation with the set designer Jaroslav Malina, for whose sets she designed costumes from the end of the 1960s, was suited to her stylistically aggressive view of theatre. With him she experienced the era of action scenography (the 1970s and 1980s) and the tendency toward the designed quality and newly transforming mannerism of the 1990s.

As a former pupil of Tröster, Franková has always had a feeling for costume which was primarily sculptural, like a three-dimensional object, capable of functioning as an equivalent component of the stage space. She chooses colors in relation to the material, shape, and dramatic function of the character, expressing through them an aggressive belligerence, a passionate accent, and humor both robust and intellectual. Her originally conceived costumes combine stylized historical attributes with fashionable contemporary elements and textile techniques. She created costumes of majestic proportions for Molière's *Don Juan*—a collection of mourning garments, royal and ostentatious, of solidified grandeur. The costumes for Sophocles' *Oedipus* (1996), supplemented by tall, almost fantastic heads, turned the chorus into majestic statues, supporting the barbaric monumentality of the architecturally conceived set by Jaroslav Malina. An example of her modeling of actors' figures into shapes that were caricatured but still human are her designs for the characters of Gogol's *The Government Inspector* (2000). The playful and cruelly joking deformations, supported by an ironically cheerful combination of colors and the use of flexible material, turned the costumes into a pictorial anecdote underscored by quaint wigs and hats.

KAREL GLOGR

Karel Glogr, set designer, was born in Prague in 1958. From 1977 to 1982 he studied set design under Jan Dušek and Albert Pražák, both pupils of František Tröster, at the Theatre Faculty of the Academy of Performing Arts in Prague, where he himself has worked as a teacher since 2000. Work with directors of different inclinations has led him to the use of various styles and expressive media. However, in the context of a given production he maintains a unified style. He is closest to the director Hana Burešová, whose work also shows diversity in style and genre. Together they have staged both tragedies and farces, frequently with a conscious paraphrase of period production practice. In Calderon's *Miraculous Mage* (1995) Glogr used Baroque wings, liberated from their traditional illusionism; their artificiality was recognized and emphasized. The set design for Johann Nepomuk Nestroy's farce *Monkeys and Women* (1999) was, ironically, a cheap color-print idyll, complete with the use of wings.

Glogr undertook this excursion into the history of styles with other directors. In Arthur Schnitzler's *Undiscovered Country*, directed by Ladislav Smoček in 1992, he applied wing prospects whose idyllic quality contrasted with the bitter out-of-tune quality of the play. In Shakespeare's *Othello*, directed by Jan Burian in 1995, the meaning of an architectural element varied by details: a grouping of neutral rectangles was at one time rocks on the seashore, at another palaces in the city streets. In the design for J. M. R. Lenz's *Tutors*, directed by Petr Kracik in 1998, the influence of the expressionist vision of reality is recognizable: the deployment and uneasy tilt of movable elements is reminiscent of an old cemetery with tombs half overturned, and creates a disturbed, tense atmosphere.

DANA HÁVOVÁ

Dana Hávová was born in Jihlava in 1955 and is a costume designer. From 1977 to 1982 she studied in the Theatre Faculty of the Academy of Performing Arts in Prague with Albert Pražák and Jan Dušek. Her own artistic inclinations are robust exaggeration and caricature, in the spirit of which she layers costume like a superfluous peel or a protective carapace. She avoids slickness and harmony and is clearly influenced by the aesthetic of ugliness related to some aspects of action scenography. The characters in *Hodinový hotelier* (*Rooms by the Hour*) by Pavel Landovský, directed by Jan Burian in 1990, are wrapped up in their clothes as though in bullet-proof armor. They wear everyday clothes, but they look as though they are wearing a full body mask. The nod in the direction of fashion is thrown into doubt by Hávová's junk-shop hallmark. Analogous junk-shop impropriety, although less striking, marks the costumes for *Pokoušení* (*Temptation*) by Václav Havel, directed by Jan Burian in 1991. The satanic masks which the characters wear for the party are more harmonious and chic than their everyday wear, which is always a little loose-fitting, with the illusion of comfort. The caricatured enlarged heads of the designs present a comedy about society—a panoptical display of depersonalized phantoms, fulfilling the idea of a modern witches' Sabbath.

VLASTISLAV HOFMAN

Vlastislav Hofman (1884–1964) was an architect, painter, printmaker, applied artist of furniture, metalwork, and porcelain, design theoretician, and theatrical designer. He was among those Czech architects who between 1910 and 1924 uniquely made use of cubist inspiration in architecture and applied art. In this, the object was the starting model from which the creator drew typical features for his own morphology: "An ashtray can turn into a house, a house into an ashtray." In 1919 Hofman abandoned the broad spectrum of his previously cubist-influenced work and, after meeting the expressionist theatre director Karel Hugo Hilar, devoted himself exclusively to the theatre. In Prague he worked with the National Theatre and the Vinohrady Theatre. He was awarded the State Prize in 1924, the Grand Prix at the World Exhibition in Paris in 1937, and the Gran Premio at the Triennial in Milan. "If I have to talk about my nerve," he announced, "I can say only that that characteristic expressiveness which some people find in my designs is maybe caused by my frequent sullenness or something similar. It must be behind it somewhere, for otherwise no prescription exists for what is actually dramatic."

JOSEF JELÍNEK

Josef Jelínek was born in 1949 and is a graduate of the Prague Academy of Performing Arts (1968–1971) and the Bratislava High School of Performing Arts (1971–1975). Jelínek's knowledge of textile techniques and his views on the concept of theatrical costume were passed on to him mainly by Ludmila Purkyňová, a Slovak costume designer and winner of the gold medal at the Prague Quadrennial, 1967. After his graduation he was the designer for the Workers' Theatre in Zlín (formerly known as Gottwaldov), where he raised the technical and artistic level of the costume workshops and the quality of their stock. Since 1982 he has been a costume designer for the National Theatre in Prague. Although he designs for every dramatic genre, opera and ballet are closest to him. His hallmark is the characteristically inventive combination of materials alongside an expressive ability for characterization, often to the extent of mannerist embellishment.

VIKTOR KRONBAUER

Viktor Kronbauer was born in Prague in 1949 on the stage of the National Theatre (his mother was an actor). He is a photographer who has worked for the Theatre Institute in Prague and for theatres in the rest of the country. Since 1987 he has been photodocumenting the Prague Quadrennial of stage design and theatre architecture. He organizes exhibitions especially on the occasion of festivals, where he also leads workshops. He considers himself the pupil of Jaroslav

Krejčí, who recorded the important initiatives of Czech theatre by capturing the inner life or message of a moment. He learned from him how to identify the essential feature of a production in the limited moment of a photo shot. Black-and-white photography has the power of concentration; contrast, composition, picture, and space excel in it. Kronbauer's photographs capture moments when "something important" is happening, is absorbed into the sequence of action in space, or "something" lurks in that space to apply its action-shaping power. Shakespeare's *Richard III*, directed by Vladimír Morávek and staged in the Globe Theatre in Prague (for whose record in photographs he won the silver medal at the Triennial in Nový Sad in Serbia in 2002) is captured in an atmosphere of tension around the key moments, and with a sense for the stylization of the acting in the costumes of Sylva Zimula Hanáková. For the audience, photography cannot replace the experience of seeing a production, but it can arouse interest and the desire to view the other worlds of the theatre.

JAROSLAV MALINA

Jaroslav Malina, born in Prague in 1937, is a set and costume designer, a painter, printmaker, and teacher. He studied from 1957 to 1961 in the Faculty of Education of the Charles University in Prague, and from 1961 to 1964 in the department of stage design of the Theatre Faculty of the Academy of Performing Arts in Prague with František Tröster, later teaching there himself (1990–2000) and serving as rector (1996–1999). He was also a private pupil of Zdeněk Sklenář, whose imaginative painting influenced Malina greatly. He has served as a professor at universities in the United States, Japan, Finland, and Great Britain, where he received an honorary doctorate from Nottingham Trent University (2002). In 1991, 1999, and 2003 he was the general commissioner of the Prague Quadrennial. His activities at home and abroad include four hundred designs for theatre, film, and television, thirty one-person exhibitions (scenography, paintings, graphics, posters), and dozens of group exhibitions, for which he has won numerous awards including the gold medal at the Seventh International Triennial of Stage Design in Nový Sad, Serbia (1984).

Malina's artworks are in the collections of the National Gallery, National Museum, Museum of Decorative Arts, Museum of Czech Music, and Theatre Institute (all in Prague), as well as the Ohio State University Theatre Research Institute, the Performing Arts Library and Museum in San Francisco, the Tobin Theatre Arts Fund of San Antonio, the Sasakawa Peace Foundation, and in many private collections. His works have frequently been published in professional magazines and were featured in *Stage Design* (Tony Davis, 2001) and in the monograph *Jaroslav Malina*, edited by Jan Dvořák. He is the designer of the expressively fantastic visual stylization of the film *Straka v hrsti* (*Magpie in Hand*, 1982, directed by Juraj Herz), banned under communist totalitarianism. He also designs the posters for his films and theatre productions, which in a confrontation between the design renderings and their realization round off a statement about the visual appearance of the theme of the play.

As a representative of action scenography of the 1970s and 1980s Malina excelled in researching and using the special qualities of a variety of materials, integrating them in both costume and set designs. He made use especially of moldable and shapeable draperies, with the help of which he achieved an imaginative variability of the environment, counting on the audience's powers of imagination. He always let himself be inspired by the space in which he worked. At first he had his doubts about the proscenium-arch stage but later incorporated its architecture into his work. During his action period he had used elements of painted and pasteboard scenery, which through irony and paraphrase upset stylistic unity and metaphorically drew attention to the ambiguity of the world. From the end of the 1980s the painted and artificial element has appeared in his work ever more intensively, as has a visual concept of composition of the whole picture of the stage (the inspiration of reappraised Baroque illusionism). The principle of play, irony, and paraphrase does not disappear.

Some motifs have appeared in Malina's stage design throughout his work, for example, the screen/wall. A synthesis of Malina's current approach can be seen in the wall design for Per Olof Enquist's *Lynx's Hour* (2003) (MALI02–03). This setting links the authenticity (use of real things) of the seventies and the visually aestheticized concepts of the nineties. The earthy structure of the wall and the outlines of a constellation on a blue base associate the two basic areas of life—earth and sky.

DAVID MAREK

David Marek, a set and interior designer, was born in Prague in 1965. From 1985 to 1989 he studied stage design in the Theatre Faculty of the Academy of Performing Arts under Albert Pražák and Jan Dušek. In 2003 he was the commissioner of the Czech exhibit at the Prague

Quadrennial. His work is inspired by various architectural, design, and theatrical styles, but unlike the postmodernists who mixed elements of different styles and epochs in a single production, for the most part he uses only one style for each project. In the stage design for Goethe's *Clavigo* (1991) (MARE06) he used unambiguously recognizable cubist morphology, including movables.

Whereas in the 1920s broken, restless lines and shapes on the Czech stage (the expressionism and cubo-futurism of Vlastislav Hofman) were used as disturbing, dramatizing elements, at the beginning of the 1990s the reappearance of the style operated as a postmodern recollection. During the 1990s Marek freed himself from such directly used influences, but, on the other hand, his share in the scenic interpretation of a work increased, chiefly in cooperation with the director Michal Dočekal. For Chekhov's *Three Sisters* (1996) Marek and Dočekal created a space by using elements of monumental palace architecture, sharpened in a dreamlike way with the help of light; the scenic interpretation allowed the sisters as old women to relive their story in their distorted memories somewhere in a Soviet old people's home. At the beginning of the new millennium spatial sensitivity began to appear more strikingly in his work. The stage design for the opera *Bloud* (*The Artless*) by Josef Bohuslav Foerster (2002) is founded on the articulation of the stage floor—gradually rising pathways as the motif of a journey, here the journey to God's tomb—and the effectiveness of the backcloth beyond the emptied space: the black silhouettes of the characters on the dawn blue horizon, fatefully watching out, are a tableau—a part of the set design.

PETR MATÁSEK

Petr Matásek, a designer of puppets, sets, and costumes, as well as a teacher, was born in Prague 1944. From 1962 to 1966 he studied stage design for puppetry in the Theatre Faculty of the Academy of Performing Arts in Prague, where in 1992 he became a teacher in the department for alternative and puppet theatre. He shared in the revival of modern Czech puppet theatre, beginning in the 1960s and fully developed in the 1970s. He did not conceive of the stage as a flat picture but as a space whose three-dimensional quality is used for the play of both a puppet and a live actor—the puppet-player, who is not a mere hidden string-puller but a partner of the puppet. Apart from the puppet, a costume and mask were also incorporated into puppet stage design. A central object was asserted as the basic scenic element—a neutrally and concretely conceived construction, animated by the puppet and the live actor, and by means of their actions capable of variable changes. The use of authentic materials and objects, and the actor's work with the object—in this case, the puppet—links Matásek's work with action scenography.

To make his puppets Matásek uses various materials and techniques. His favorite material is wood, which with its living essence and individual structure has always been a magical material for him. Many of his puppets are inspired by the Czech folk carvers' tradition of expressive deep carving, to which is added the imagination, poetry, and humor of this contemporary artist, who nevertheless stamps individual expression on his products.

Matásek has been working in the field of straight drama since the 1980s and has enriched it with the resourceful approaches and liberated fantasy of the puppet theatre. More recently he has involved himself in the use of nontraditional stages. For Christopher Marlowe's *Faust* he adapted the underground stone hall of Gorlice (2001), used as a depository for the original Baroque statues from the Charles Bridge, and equipped this space with simple objects of an almost ritual nature. In 2003 he created a project called Bouda ("Hut"—the affectionate term for the first purpose-built Czech-language theatre in the early nineteenth century). It was not only a design, but also a conceptual initiative serving as an alternative stage for one season for the National Theatre. In a purist toy-brick structure, installed in the square behind the National Theatre company's Theatre of the Estates, actors and audience experienced the performance as though they were all in the hold of a ship, thus literally in the same boat.

MIROSLAV MELENA

Melena, born in 1937, is a graduate of the art education department of the Faculty of Education of Charles University and the Theatre Faculty of the Academy of Performing Arts in Prague and a pupil of František Tröster. From 1965 to 1969 Melena was designer at the Petr Bezruč Theatre in Ostrava and from 1980 to 1981 head of design at the theatre in Maribor in Yugoslavia. Since 1962 he has worked mainly with Jan Schmid, theatre director, writer, and designer, and head of the famous Liberec (and later Prague) theatre Studio Ypsilon. Collaboration with Schmid has left its mark on Melena's poetics and sharpened his sense of humor for the paradoxical confrontation of different realities of life. He has systematically devoted himself to theatre architecture as the designer of laminated-shell summer theatres (Yugoslavia) and co-designer of the reconstruction of Czech theatres in the nineties and beyond. Among his most important projects have been the reconstruction of the theatre in Jihlava and in Prague the rebuilding of the Archa Theatre and the reconstruction of the Fidlovačka Theatre. Since 1998 he has lectured at the Janáček Academy of Performing Arts in Brno.

JANA PREKOVÁ

Jana Preková, born in 1956, is a set and costume designer. In 1983 she graduated from the Theatre Faculty of the Academy of Performing Arts in Prague, where she was a pupil of Jan Dušek, Albert Pražák, and Irena Greifová. She works with a permanent circle of directors, mainly Jan Nebeský (Prague Municipal Theatres) and later Jan Antonín Pitínský. Her set designs grow out of symbols; the dramatic reality of set and costume is conveyed in the magic ritual of sign language. Since 1990 she has been lecturing in the design department of the Janáček Academy of Performing Arts in Brno and in 1996 became head of the department; in 1998 she received the title of docent (assistant professor). Her method of work and her artistic views have helped to form the expressive profile of the school.

MARTA ROSZKOPFOVÁ

Marta Roszkopfová was born in Žilina (Slovakia) in 1947 and is a set and costume designer as well as a printmaker. She studied from 1968 to 1973 at the High School of Performing Arts in Bratislava under Ladislav Vychodil and Ludmila Purkyňová and from 1973 to 1974 at the Akademii sztuk pieknych in Warsaw under Józef Szajna and Zenobiusz Strzelecki. In 1974 she became designer at the Petr Bezruč Theatre in Ostrava, where she has worked on a dramaturgically challenging repertory, while having established herself in a number of other theatres. In 1984 and in 1998 she won the gold medal at the Triennial of Stage Design in Nový Sad in Serbia. Her roughened view of world drama is not unconnected with the less than idyllic Ostrava landscape, an industrial mining region. The influence of Polish theatre of the 1960s and 1970s, which linked an expressive vision with an "aesthetic ugliness," can be recognized in her work, especially at the beginning. A liking for authentic material and the functional liberation of the stage, as well as an emphasis on the visual and metaphorical power of costume, brings her close to the practice of action scenography. Her costumes are filled by robust bodies who, so to speak, shape them and overflow them. The morphological aggressiveness of the costume (in detail as in color) is visually attractive and emotionally repulsive.

Roszkopfová puts an everyday element into effect in historical costumes, while she makes contemporary costumes special by using comic exaggeration. The costumes for *Accidental Death of an Anarchist* by Dario Fo (1989) are mundane in nature, but layered on the actors like protective and combative masks. In the costumes for Shakespeare's *Twelfth Night* (1998) the designer comes surprisingly to an almost provocative sobriety, given the carnival nature of the comedy, which is only mildly enlivened by stylized detail.

In conceiving set design Roszkopfová is more sober in color and shape. She has accustomed us to a rather neutrally conceived set. However, she knows how to surprise, by plasticity in shape, for example. The castle Elsinor in the drawing of designs for Shakespeare's *Hamlet* (1999) is a forked shape, reminiscent of the stump of a centuries-old tree beheaded by lightning. The restless forming of this shape and its material concentration on the center of the stage suggest an unwitting echo of expressionism.

SIMONA RYBÁKOVÁ

Simona Rybáková, born in 1963, is a costume designer and author of projects for theatre, film, and television. Rybáková graduated from the School of Applied Arts in Prague in 1981 and from the High School of Applied Arts in Prague in 1991, in the field of textile design. After a year at the Helsinki University of Industrial Art, she studied at the Rhode Island School of Design. Rybáková designed costumes and danced in the amateur ballet company Křeč, a part of the famous company known as the Prague Five, which at the turn of the 1980s and 1990s combined theatre, dance, design, film, and television. Since 1990 she has worked with the architect and designer Daniel Dvořák, former artistic director of the State Opera in Prague and the National Theatre. She designs costumes for television and since 1995 has been costume designer for the International Film Festival in Karlovy Vary. In 1995 she won the Swarowski Award. She uses the exaggerated mannerism of her costumes and wigs critically, as an instrument of irony.

OTAKAR SCHINDLER

Otakar Schindler (1923–1998) was a theatrical designer and painter. A graduate of the School of Applied Arts in Prague and a pupil of Emil Filla, a Czech cubist painter, Schindler was a member of the generation that entered the theatre with a background in fine art. He began working in Ostrava in the 1950s, where up to 1975 he was head of design at the Petr Bezruč Theatre. Until 1990 he was head of design at the Realist Theatre in Prague, and from then on worked as a freelance. When in 1976 Jan Kačer began to work with the Emil František Burian Theatre in Prague and the State Theatre in Ostrava, Kačer became, along with Luboš Pistorius at the Realist Theatre, Schindler's most important director colleague. Schindler captured several stylistic eras in his work —the major period of grand visual scenography of the 1940s, the formal euphoria of the 1970s, and action scenography. He also reacted to end-of-the century retro design.

JAN SLÁDEK

Jan Sládek (1906–1982) was a theatrical designer, painter, and printmaker who spent his youth in Ostrava, in a mining colony. His humble family beginnings, and the fact that his subsistence and upbringing depended on his mother's going out to work, determined his choice of a career as a clerk; he studied painting and the history of art privately. In 1930 he was invited by the director Jan Škoda to work with him in the National Theatre of Moravia and Silesia in Ostrava; from 1931 he worked with the Slovak National Theatre in Bratislava, and from 1936 with the Regional Theatre in Brno. During 1937–1944 he worked with the Vinohrady Theatre in Prague and in 1938 designed his first production for the National Theatre in Prague. After World War II, he founded the Realist Theatre in Prague with the directors Jan Škoda and Karel Palouš, and remained there until 1979. Influenced by expressionism and abstractionism, he created environments sensitively treated through color and light. In 1937 he received the gold medal at the Triennial in Milan.

KATEŘINA ŠTEFKOVÁ

Kateřina Štefková was born in Prague in 1971 and is a costume and set designer. From 1989 to 1994 she studied stage design at the Theatre Faculty of the Academy of Performing Arts in Prague under Jaroslav Malina and Jan Dušek. She has been designer for the Theatre on the Balustrade in Prague since 1994. Her work is marked by the visually accented vision of the director Petr Lébl (1963–1999; artistic director of the Theatre on the Balustrade, 1993–1999), full of disturbing images, beautiful on the outside, anxious within. A knowledge of the history of clothing and textiles facilitates her freedom in thinking out fantastic creations. The care and thoroughness with which she chooses details and different clothing techniques is married to irrationality and the strangeness of varied combinations. Even her "ordinary" costumes are, in connection with the acting and the director's interpretation, something special and improper. She uses quotes from different styles of clothing, in accord with the wave of postmodernism, as elements which particularize and interpret. The female protagonist of Tankred Dorst's *Fernando Krapp Wrote Me a Letter* (1989) was displayed like an opera character in a mannerist frame with a lush Secession setting, not so the director and designer could place the play in a certain period, but to make clear the exceptional quality and theatricality of the fate of a single human. The colorfully profligate, operatically decorated *Government Inspector* (1995), shifted by costume stylization into "barbarian" Asia, forced on the audience a completely unusual and shocking view of a notoriously over-familiar play, thereby provoking unaccustomed associations. That also applied to Lébl's series of plays by Chekhov (*The Seagull*, 1994, Alfréd Radok Award for the best production of the year; *Ivanov*, 1997; *Uncle Vanya*, 1999). Here the costumes were stylized more subtly, chiefly through color, but as part of a crystallized whole they particularized the world of the production through unusual viewpoints, with elements of silent film, Russian romanticism, and the American Western.

ZUZANA ŠTEFUNKOVÁ

Štefunková, born in 1970, is a costume designer. She graduated from the Secondary School of Applied Arts in Uherské Hradiště in 1988 and the Theatre Faculty of the Academy of Performing Arts in Prague in 1995. At the latter she studied in the department of alternative and puppet theatre, where she was a pupil of Pavel Kalfus and Irena Marečková. Štefunková has worked with the Dejvice Theatre in Prague and the HaTheatre in Brno. She designed the costumes for the dramatic text *Sister Anxiety*, based on poems by Jakub Deml and Jan Čep, and for Henry Purcell's opera *Dido and Aeneas*, both of which were directed by Jan Antonin Pitínský and won the Alfréd Radok awards for the best Czech production of the year in 1996 and 1999, respectively.

JAN ŠTĚPÁNEK

Jan Štěpánek, born in Prague in 1970, is a set designer. He returned to Czechoslovakia from Germany after the end of communism, and from 1992 to 1998 studied stage design at the Theatre Faculty of the Academy of Performing Arts in Prague under Jan Dušek. He worked for small and large theatres, but exclusively with directors with whom he felt an affinity. He was influenced by the rawness of German theatre. His designs of sombre and aggressive colors are worlds in themselves—expressive and emotional images which apparently have nothing in common with the theatrical stage. In fact, they suggest the spirit of the production, or at least the designer's idea of it. In outdoor locations we often see austerity and asceticism in Štěpánek's sets, but something of the original pictorial vision penetrates, especially by means of lighting, as though the designer determined the theme of the play for himself and in his designs transposes it into visual art. *People Annihilation* by Werner Schwab (1999) is a picturesque danse macabre, in which luscious colors appear from materials of darkness. The Hanged Men in Marius von Mayerburg's *Fireface* (2000) have the shape of dead fish, with decoratively ornamented, emptied interiors like rare drawings in India ink. Some sort of ritual agony is abstractly expressed in the designs for Gabriela Preissová's *Gazdina roba* (*Household Woman*, 2000), the urgency of the basic dramatic quality of the theme resounding all the more intensely.

PETRA ŠTĚTINOVÁ GOLDFLAMOVÁ

Petra Štětinová Goldflamová, born in Prague in 1970, is a costume, set, and puppet designer. From 1990 to 1996 she studied set design in the department of alternative and puppet theatre of the Theatre Faculty of the Academy of Performing Arts in Prague under Petr Matásek and Miroslav Melena. The schooling in puppetry is not irrelevant to her work. In the production *Kdyby prase mělo křídla* (*If Pigs Had Wings*, 1996) puppet animals appeared, even though this was not a puppet production but a cabaret with songs for children. They were part of the whole theatrical picture book, supporting by resourceful visual expression the imagination of the child audience. Recently the designer has created costumes for productions by the director Arnošt Goldflam. She approaches the figure in costume and mask with tenderness and humor, as though it were a puppet. Her designs are reminiscent of illustrations for fairy stories. Imagination surrounds her like a beneficial background and forms concrete shapes with irony and joy. *Cabaret Vian-Cami* (1998) was full of peculiar beings, jokey and a little dangerous—from Neanderthals to archaized pilots. Her designs for the straight theatre version of Puccini's *La Bohème* by Arnošt Goldflam (2002) are lyrically ironic without caricatured exaggeration; dove gray and pink flowers glow on Mimi with a subtle harmony, not very typical for contemporary Czech theatre.

JOSEF SVOBODA

Josef Svoboda (1920–2002) was a graduate of the School of Applied Arts in Prague, where he became professor in 1969. He was head of design at a number of leading Prague theatres: the Grand Opera of the Fifth of May, the National Theatre, and Laterna Magika. He was one of the most important international stage designers of the second half of the twentieth century. In 1993 a monograph on Svoboda by Jarka Burian was published in both Europe and America. He lectured and worked with directors and choreographers in theatres on every continent, and he collaborated with Laurence Olivier, Giorgio Strehler, Leonard Bernstein, and others. He was awarded numerous major international honors, created new approaches to stage design, and earned technological patents. He introduced the polyecran system on stage, as well as lasers and holographs, and made use of the techniques of optics, kinetics, and electronics. Svoboda believed set design to be a flexible and dynamic element that helps to determine the meaning of the production. In his words, "the basis of the theatrical performance has for a long time not been the dramatic text, but the scenario, the result of the coming together of direction and stage design."

EGON TOBIÁŠ

Egon Tobiáš, born in Kladno in 1971, is a playwright, poet, set designer, and printmaker. From 1989 to 1995 he studied stage design at the Theatre Faculty of the Academy of Performing Arts in Prague under Jaroslav Malina; as a postgraduate, he studied book illustration and printmaking with Jiří Šalamoun. He works in the print studio Hamlet and created the logo of the Theatre Institute in Prague. Although he graduated as a stage designer, he practices as such only sporadically. His plays have appeared on Czech stages more often than his designs. He is fascinated by the theatre as a world unto itself with its own set of rules separate from quotidian reality. As a contemporary artist he draws on the past, adapting to his pictures the impulses of Secession, decadence, symbolism, and expressionism. He is a set designer of the picture rather than of space; he has his own world, in which are linked poetry, visual art, and theatre. For *Sestra Úzkost* (*Sister Anxiety*), a stage poem by Jan Čep, Jakub Deml, and J. A. Pitínský (1995, Alfréd Radok Award for the best production of the year), he created a ritual space, conceived with symbolic imagery—rustic, concrete, dreamily eerie. The realization and designs differ, but are in both cases steeped in a muted mysticism and poetry. His set designs for the play by Jane Bowles *In the Summerhouse* were provocatively painted and deliberately archaic; the main elements of the set were the alternating backcloths in whose luscious strokes we can observe echoes of expressionism.

FRANTIŠEK TRÖSTER

František Tröster was born in Vrbičance u Roudnice in 1904 and died in Prague in 1968. He was a set designer, architect, urban planner, and teacher. He studied from 1924 to 1928 at the School of Architecture and Construction in Prague, and from 1928 to 1931 he continued to study architecture at the School of Applied Arts in Prague under Pavel Janák, an architect of Czech cubism. From 1934 to 1938 he taught at the School of Arts and Crafts in Bratislava (Slovakia) and from 1939 to 1943 in the Central School of Interior Design in Prague. He began to teach stage design in 1943 at the State Conservatoire in Prague. From 1948 to 1968 he was head of the department of stage design at the Theatre Faculty of the Academy of Performing Arts in Prague.

As an architect Tröster created installations for exhibitions, often at an international level; he shared in the creation of the Czechoslovak pavilion at EXPO 58 in Brussels. At the Biennial of Visual Arts in São Paulo in Brazil in 1959 he was awarded the gold medal in the stage design section for the best foreign stage designer. In the 1920s he designed sets for amateur theatres and later worked with the Moderní studio in Prague, founded by Jiří Frejka, one of the most important Czech theatre directors of the twentieth century. In the 1930s he worked with the progressive theatre designer Viktor Šulc in the Slovak National Theatre in Bratislava, and in the National Theatre in Prague again with Jiří Frejka, who brought the untraditional approaches of the avant-garde theatres to the official stage and for a long period became Tröster's close collaborator.

In 1944 Tröster was discriminated against by the Nazi occupiers and forced to work under aliases. With Frejka he worked by a method of hyperbolic realism, which arose from the realities of the time but transformed them through artistic means, structured them anew, and emphasized them by abbreviation and hyperbole. He concerned himself with the dramatic relationship of space and time. In his concept every play had its own space, its own cosmos, which went beyond the dimensions of the stage and was represented on it by the three-dimensional elements of light and movement, that is, the actor's performance. The components of the space reacted dynamically to the movement of the action and the actors' performance and transformed themselves.

After World War II there was a particular development in Tröster's work with light. In *Les Nuits de la colère* by Armand Salacrou (*Nights of Anger*, 1947), clashing walls changed their meaning (viaduct, interior, prison) through the lighting. The change of meaning of the originally neutral object will later play an important role in what is known as action scenography. In a production of Alban Berg's opera *Wozzek* (1959), asymmetrically arranged screens served as surfaces on which could be projected images of individual locations having features of expressionist agitation—for example, apartment blocks, a lake, a police station. The painted screen walls, when illuminated from behind, became transparent and seemed like steamed-up glass in a poverty-stricken interior.

JAN VANČURA

Jan Vančura, born in 1940, is a graduate of the Industrial Glass College in Železný Brod and the Academy of Applied Arts in Prague. He has done most of his stage design work for the F.X. Šalda Theatre in Liberec and the South Bohemian Theatre in České Budějovice, the Provincial Theatre in Brno, and the Prague National Theatre. Vančura won a silver medal at the 1979 Prague Quadrennial. The designs he exhibited were not functional, which is a primary requirement for action scenography. For Vančura, the environment of the drama always is a grandiose picture. His work is essentially decorative but some of his romantic, classically painted scenery seems to be riveted from sheet metal. While his work as a whole tends toward the past, there are details that place it in our time, emphasizing the conflict between the needs of former times and the experience of 20th-century man.

JANA ZBOŘILOVÁ

Jana Zbořilová, set and costume designer, was born in Prague in 1952. From 1972 to 1974 she studied stage design under Michael Romberg and Albert Pražák (a pupil of František Tröster) at the Theatre Faculty of the Academy of Performing Arts in Prague, where she has been teaching since 1990. In 2001 she won the gold medal at the Triennial of Stage Design in Nový Sad in Serbia. She is influenced by the openness, objectivity, and variability of action scenography and the related imaginative aesthetics of the Brno Theatre Goose on a String, with which she worked in the 1970s. Her collaborations with this poetically inspired studio theatre (director Eva Tálská) were full of tenderness and cruelty, but also inventive humor in *Kytice* [Nosegay], *Píseň o Viktorce* [Song of Viktorka], and *Šibeniční písně* [Gallows Songs]. When the theme requires it, her humor can become sarcastic to the point of merciless incrimination, especially in the costume element. A sense for comic and poetic playfulness also operates on large stages, where it is combined with the simultaneous need for the gesture of monumental shape and dramatic pathos. This combination has proved important at the National Theatre in Brno, for example, in collaboration with director Zdeněk Kaloč in the 1990s.

There is in Zbořilová's designs an inexhaustible sense of humor and play with subjects and meanings, manifested in diverse nuances. These impulses can be detected in her use of collage for some of her set designs (Chekhov's *Uncle Vanya*, 1996, Molière's *Misanthrope*, 1998, and Marivaux's *Le Dispute*, 2002). Her work forms a link proceeding from the poetism of the 1920s, the Czech period of surrealism, to film montage, through the material and objective diversity of 1960s visual art, and, finally, to the "cut and paste" aesthetic of postmodernism. The resultant costume creations focus on grotesque parody, chiefly in the female characters, who are captured with a devastating lack of flattery. Zbořilová's designs for Eva Tálská's *Se mnou kůň a smrt* (*Horse and Death with Me*, 1999) exemplify this point. In the play, subtle clowns are endowed with a nostalgic poetry (ZBOR03); however, the female clown is portrayed as a hyperbolized caricature of a bogus wrestler (ZBOR04).

IVO ŽÍDEK

Ivo Žídek, a set designer, was born in Ostrava in 1948. From 1968 to 1970 he studied stage design at the Theatre Faculty of the Academy of Performing Arts in Prague, where he was one of the last pupils of František Tröster, and from 1971 to 1974 at the School of Applied Arts under Josef Svoboda. His work is not far from action scenography or from Tröster's three-dimensional space. He has worked for both small and large theatres, including the National Theatre in Prague, and is a sought-after stage designer for operettas and musicals. The high point of his work was with the Theatre on the Balustrade in Prague and its artistic director, the intellectually demanding Jan Grossman. The influence of Žídek's brief period of study with Tröster was manifested on this small stage, which has asserted progressive tendencies in the theatre ever since its founding in 1958.

In Molière's *Don Juan* (1989) the central structurally conceived object occupied most of the stage space. This concrete fragment of a monument of architecture changed its meaning, atmosphere, and functions in connection with the action and the actors' performance. The eerily enlarged and narrowed doors in Václav Havel's autobiographical *Largo Desolato* (1990) surrounded the comings and goings of private individuals like ramparts of silent but ever-present spies. At the same time they created a projection screen for the play of the deformed shadow of an antique chandelier whose arms/tentacles made visible the eeriness of the nightmares of the spied-on dissident protagonist. The central accent of the stage design for productions of another play by Havel, *Pokoušení* (*Temptation*, the Faust theme updated to 1991), was a round opening in an expressively angled ceiling under which were placed a bucket and a washbasin. It served as a passage for raids by the devil and was at the same time an ordinary, uncomfortable hole, through which water dripped—a clear use of metaphor and irony.

SYLVA ZIMULA HANÁKOVÁ

Sylva Zimula Hanáková, born in Kroměříž in 1967, is a costume and set designer. From 1986 to 1991 she studied in the Faculty of Education of the Masaryk University in Brno and, from 1991 to 1992, stage design at the Janáček Academy of Performing Arts in Brno under Jan Konečný. She has designed costumes for different types of companies and different genres. She attracted attention to herself chiefly by her work with Vladimír Morávek, a director of striking visual fantasies. In a production of Shakespeare's *Richard III* directed by Morávek and staged in the Globe Theatre—the Prague replica of the Elizabethan London stage—her costumes share in carrying an inventive gaudy layer of the production, attracting the attention of the "crowd" (the audience), which was distracted by background noise from the nearby amusement park at Výstaviště (exhibition ground), the location of the Prague Quadrennial. The effectiveness of the costumes, however, relied on the actor. It was only with the goblinlike physical gestures of Richard (Pavel Zedníček, Miroslav Donutil) that Richard's short black cloak and clownishly extended gloves acquired meaning. The elegant manners of the male actors, performing the female characters according to Elizabethan practices, were essential for the royal majesty of the costumes to resound fully.

LIST OF CD IMAGES

NUMBER	DESIGNER	PRODUCTION	MEDIUM	DATE	VENUE
ANYZ01	Helena Anýžová	Bastien and Bastienne	Costume	1999	National Theatre of Moravia and Silesia, Ostrava
ANYZ02	Helena Anýžová	Paris Plays First Fiddle	Costume	2002	National Theatre of Moravia and Silesia, Ostrava, at Hukvaldy Castle
ANYZ03	Helena Anýžová	Paris Plays First Fiddle	Costume	2002	National Theatre of Moravia and Silesia, Ostrava, at Hukvaldy Castle
ANYZ04	Helena Anýžová	Paris Plays First Fiddle	Costume	2002	National Theatre of Moravia and Silesia, Ostrava, at Hukvaldy Castle
ANYZ05	Helena Anýžová	Paris Plays First Fiddle	Costume	2002	National Theatre of Moravia and Silesia, Ostrava, at Hukvaldy Castle
DUSE01	Jan Dušek	Too Loud a Solitude	Scenic	1984	Theatre on the Balustrade, Prague
DUSE02	Jan Dušek	The Play on Love, Death, and Eternity	Scenic	1998	Municipal Theatre, Brno
DUSE03	Jan Dušek	The Play on Love, Death, and Eternity	Scenic	1998	Municipal Theatre, Brno
DUSE04	Jan Dušek	The Play on Love, Death, and Eternity	Scenic	1998	Municipal Theatre, Brno
DUSE05	Jan Dušek	The Master and Margarita	Scenic	1999	Municipal Theatre, Brno
DUSE06	Jan Dušek	Biederman and the Firebugs	Costume	1990	Theatre K, Prague
DUSE07	Jan Dušek	A Magic Hill	Scenic	1997	Dlouhá Theatre, Prague
DUSE08	Jan Dušek	Persians	Costume	2004	Strub Theatre, Loyola Marymount University, Los Angeles
DUSE09	Jan Dušek	Persians	Costume	2004	Strub Theatre, Loyola Marymount University, Los Angeles

NUMBER	DESIGNER	PRODUCTION	MEDIUM	DATE	VENUE
DUSE10	Jan Dušek	Persians	Costume	2004	Strub Theatre, Loyola Marymount University, Los Angeles
FRAN01	Marie Franková	Oedipus Rex	Costume	1996	National Theatre (Theatre of the Estates), Prague
FRAN02	Marie Franková	Don Juan	Costume	1988	E. F. Burian Theatre, Prague
FRAN03	Marie Franková	The Inspector General	Costume	1999	Municipal Theatre, Zlín
FRAN04	Marie Franková	The Inspector General	Costume	1999	Municipal Theatre, Zlín
FRAN05	Marie Franková	The Inspector General	Costume	1999	Municipal Theatre, Zlín
GLOG01	Karel Glogr	Richard III	Scenic	1999	Tyl Theatre, Plzeň
GLOG02	Karel Glogr	The Tutor	Scenic	1998	Theatre Pod Palmovkou, Prague
GLOG03	Karel Glogr	August August, August	Scenic	1990	Stibor Theatre, Olomouc
GLOG04	Karel Glogr	August August, August	Scenic	1990	Stibor Theatre, Olomouc
HAVO01	Dana Hávová	Temptation	Costume	1990	Tyl Theatre, Plzeň
HAVO02	Dana Hávová	Temptation	Costume	1990	Tyl Theatre, Plzeň
HAVO03	Dana Hávová	Temptation	Costume	1990	Tyl Theatre, Plzeň
HAVO04	Dana Hávová	Temptation	Costume	1990	Tyl Theatre, Plzeň
HAVO05	Dana Hávová	Temptation	Costume	1990	Tyl Theatre, Plzeň
HAVO06	Dana Hávová	Temptation	Costume	1990	Tyl Theatre, Plzeň
HAVO07	Dana Hávová	Temptation	Costume	1990	Tyl Theatre, Plzeň
HAVO08	Dana Hávová	Temptation	Costume	1990	Tyl Theatre, Plzeň
HAVO09	Dana Hávová	Temptation	Costume	1990	Tyl Theatre, Plzeň
HAVO10	Dana Hávová	Temptation	Costume	1990	Tyl Theatre, Plzeň
HOFM01	Vlastislav Hofman	The Tempest	Scenic	1920	Vinohrady Theatre, Prague
HOFM02	Vlastislav Hofman	Queen Christine	Scenic	1922	Vinohrady Theatre, Prague
HOFM03	Vlastislav Hofman	Dawn	Scenic	1920	Vinohrady Theatre, Prague
JELI01	Josef Jelínek	The Bartered Bride	Costume	1997	Slovak National Theatre, Bratislava, Slovakia
JELI02	Josef Jelínek	The Bartered Bride	Costume	1997	Slovak National Theatre, Bratislava, Slovakia
JELI03	Josef Jelínek	Macbeth	Costume	1984	National Theatre, Nová Scéna, Prague
MALI01	Jaroslav Malina	Le Dispute	Scenic	1999	Tyl Theatre, Plzeň
MALI02	Jaroslav Malina	A Lynx's Hour	Scenic	2003	Theatre Aréna, Bratislava, Slovakia
MALI03	Jaroslav Malina	A Lynx's Hour	Scenic	2003	Theatre Aréna, Bratislava, Slovakia
MALI04	Jaroslav Malina	Bacchae of Euripides	Scenic	2003	Clarence Brown Theatre, University of Tennessee, Knoxville
MALI05	Jaroslav Malina	The Inspector General	Scenic	1999	Municipal Theatre, Zlín
MALI06	Jaroslav Malina	Tartuffe	Scenic	1997–99	Municipal Theatre, Zlín

NUMBER	DESIGNER	PRODUCTION	MEDIUM	DATE	VENUE
MALI07	Jaroslav Malina	Come Nasce il Sogetto Cinematografico	Scenic	1998	Municipal Theatre, Zlín
MALI08	Jaroslav Malina	Good	Scenic	2003	Jerwood Vanbrugh Theatre, Royal Academy of Dramatic Art, London
MALI09	Jaroslav Malina	Vassa	Costume	1986	National Theatre, Prague
MALI10	Jaroslav Malina	Miss Julie	Scenic	1988	National Theatre, Nová Scéna, Prague
MALI11	Jaroslav Malina	Ballad of the Sad Café	Scenic	1987	E. F. Burian Theatre, Prague
MARE01	David Marek	The Artless	Scenic	2001	Tyl Theatre, Plzeň
MARE02	David Marek	The Artless	Scenic	2001	Tyl Theatre, Plzeň
MARE03	David Marek	The Artless	Scenic	2001	Tyl Theatre, Plzeň
MARE04	David Marek	Clavigo	Scenic	1994	Theatre Spolek Kašpar, Prague
MATA01	Petr Matásek	The Little Mermaid	Puppet	1988	Odensee Theatre, Denmark
MATA02	Petr Matásek	The Red Shoes	Costume	2003	Sogusvuntan Theatre, Reykjavik, Iceland
MATA03	Petr Matásek	The Red Shoes	Costume	2003	Sogusvuntan Theatre, Reykjavik, Iceland
MATA04	Petr Matásek	The Red Shoes	Costume	2003	Sogusvuntan Theatre, Reykjavik, Iceland
MATA05	Petr Matásek	The Little Mermaid	Costume	1988	Odensee Theatre, Denmark
MATA06	Petr Matásek	Cirkus Unikum	Puppet	1978	Drak Theatre, Hradec Králové
MATA07	Petr Matásek	Cirkus Unikum	Puppet	1978	Drak Theatre, Hradec Králové
MATA08	Petr Matásek	Cirkus Unikum	Puppet	1978	Drak Theatre, Hradec Králové
MATA09	Petr Matásek	Don Quixote	Puppet	1994	Drak Theatre, Hradec Králové
MATA10	Petr Matásek	Don Quixote	Puppets, in situ	1994	Drak Theatre, Hradec Králové
MATA11	Petr Matásek	Cirkus Unikum	Puppet	1978	Drak Theatre, Hradec Králové
MATA12	Petr Matásek	Don Quixote	Puppet	1994	Drak Theatre, Hradec Králové
MELE01	Miroslav Melena	The Caretaker	Scenic	1990	Studio Ypsilon, Prague
MELE02	Miroslav Melena	The Twelve Chairs	Scenic	1973	Studio Ypsilon, Liberec
PREK01	Jana Preková	Preková Exhibition	Installation	1999	PQ99
ROSZ01	Marta Roszkopfová	Accidental Death of An Anarchist	Costume	1989	Bezruč Theatre, Ostrava
ROSZ02	Marta Roszkopfová	Accidental Death of An Anarchist	Costume	1989	Bezruč Theatre, Ostrava
ROSZ03	Marta Roszkopfová	Peer Gynt	Scenic	2002	Silesian Theatre, Opava
ROSZ04	Marta Roszkopfová	Copenhagen	Scenic	2000	Šalda Theatre, Liberec

NUMBER	DESIGNER	PRODUCTION	MEDIUM	DATE	VENUE
ROSZ05	Marta Roszkopfová	Hamlet	Scenic	1999	Bezruč Theatre, Ostrava
ROSZ06	Marta Roszkopfová	Romeo and Juliet	Scenic	1988	Bezruč Theatre, Ostrava
ROSZ07	Marta Roszkopfová	Jaques and His Master	Costume	1997	Bezruč Theatre, Ostrava
ROSZ08	Marta Roszkopfová	Othello (The Possessed)	Costume	1998	National Theatre, Prague
RYBA01	Simona Rybáková	Rybaková Exhibition	Costume	1999	PQ99
SCHI01	Otakar Schindler	The Wood Demon	Scenic	1974	National Theatre, Prague
SCHI02	Otakar Schindler	Teyve the Milkman	Scenic	1990	Vinohrady Theatre, Prague
SCHI03	Otakar Schindler	All's Well That Ends Well	Scenic	1980	Drama Theatre, Hradec Králové
SLAD01	Jan Sládek	The Merchant of Venice	Scenic	1933	National Theatre of Moravia, Ostrava
SLAD02	Jan Sládek	Antony and Cleopatra	Scenic	1938	National Theatre of Moravia, Ostrava
STEF01	Kateřina Štefková	Fernando Krapp Wrote Me a Letter	Costume	1992	Theatre Labyrint, Prague
STEF02	Kateřina Štefková	Uncle Vanya	Costume	1999	Theatre on the Balustrade, Prague
STEF03	Kateřina Štefková	Uncle Vanya	Costume	1999	Theatre on the Balustrade, Prague
STEF04	Kateřina Štefková	Uncle Vanya	Costume	1999	Theatre on the Balustrade, Prague
STEF05	Kateřina Štefková	Uncle Vanya	Costume	1999	Theatre on the Balustrade, Prague
STEF06	Kateřina Štefková	The Inspector General	Costume	1995	Theatre on the Balustrade, Prague
STEF07	Kateřina Štefková	The Inspector General	In situ	1995	Theatre on the Balustrade, Prague
STEP01	Jan Štěpánek	Dybbuk	Scenic	1998	Academy of Performing Arts, Prague
STEP02	Jan Štěpánek	Šárka	Scenic	2000	Tyl Theatre, Plzeň
STEP03	Jan Štěpánek	The Summer Guests	Scenic	1999	Na Palmovce Theatre, Prague
STEP04	Jan Štěpánek	Fireface	Scenic	2001	HaTheatre, Brno
STET01	Petra Štětinová Goldflamová	The Forest Maid, or Journey to America	Costume	2003	Klicpera Theatre, Hradec Králové
STET02	Petra Štětinová Goldflamová	Matthew the Honest	Costume	2002	Dlouhá Theatre, Prague
STET03	Petra Štětinová Goldflamová	Matthew the Honest	Costume	2002	Dlouhá Theatre, Prague
STET04	Petra Štětinová Goldflamová	Matthew the Honest	Costume	2002	Dlouhá Theatre, Prague
STET05	Petra Štětinová Goldflamová	La Bohème	Costume	2002	Klicpera Theatre, Hradec Králové
STET06	Petra Štětinová Goldflamová	La Bohème	Costume	2002	Klicpera Theatre, Hradec Králové
STEZ01	Zuzana Štefunková	Job	Costume	1996	HaTheatre, Brno

NUMBER	DESIGNER	PRODUCTION	MEDIUM	DATE	VENUE
STEZ02	Zuzana Štefunková	Werther	Costume	1997	Middle Bohemian Theatre, Kladno
SVOB01	Josef Svoboda	Tristan und Isolde	Scenic	1978	Grand Theatre, Geneva
SVOB02	Josef Svoboda	The Seagull	Scenic	1988	Atelier Theatral, Louvain-la-Neuve, France
TOBI01	Egon Tobiáš	Sister Anxiety	Scenic	1995	Theatre Dejvice, Prague
TOBI02	Egon Tobiáš	In the Summer House	Scenic	2001	Theatre on the Balustrade, Prague
TOBI03	Egon Tobiáš	In the Summer House	Scenic	2001	Theatre on the Balustrade, Prague
TOBI04	Egon Tobiáš	The Foreigner	Scenic	1994	Drama Studio, Ústí nad Labem
TROS01	František Tröster	The Inspector General	Scenic	1936	National Theatre, Prague
TROS02	František Tröster	The Madwoman of Chaillot	Scenic	1948	Vinohrady Theatre, Prague
TROS03	František Tröster	Don Juan	Scenic	1957	National Theatre, Prague
TROS04	František Tröster	The Pied Piper	Scenic	1942	National Theatre, Prague
TROS05	František Tröster	Romeo and Juliet	Scenic	1938	National Theatre, Prague
TROS06	František Tröster	Richard III	Scenic	1940	Provincial Theatre, Brno
TROS07	František Tröster	The Winter's Tale	Scenic	1965	National Theatre, Prague
TROS08	František Tröster	Wozzeck	Scenic	1965	National Theatre, Prague
TROS09	František Tröster	Wozzeck	Scenic	1965	National Theatre, Prague
TROS10	František Tröster	Julius Caesar	Scenic	1936	National Theatre, Prague
TROS11	František Tröster	Julius Caesar	Scenic	1936	National Theatre, Prague
TROS12	František Tröster	The Winter's Tale	Scenic	1965	National Theatre, Prague
TROS13	František Tröster	The Winter's Tale	Scenic	1965	National Theatre, Prague
VANC01	Jan Vančura	The Indians	Scenic	1987	F. X. Šalda Theatre, Liberec
VANC02	Jan Vančura	The Marriage of Figaro	Scenic	1994	F. X. Šalda Theatre, Liberec
ZBOR01	Jana Zbořilová	The Misanthrope	Scenic	1997	Vinohrady Theatre, Prague
ZBOR02	Jana Zbořilová	The Firebird	Costume	2000	National Theatre (Theatre of the Estates), Prague
ZBOR03	Jana Zbořilová	Horse and Death with Me	Costume	1999	Theatre on a String, Brno
ZBOR04	Jana Zbořilová	Horse and Death with Me	Costume	1999	Theatre on a String, Brno
ZBOR05	Jana Zbořilová	The Beggar's Opera	Costume	1990	Drama Club Theatre, Prague
ZIDE01	Ivo Žídek	Temptation	Scenic	1991	Theatre on the Balustrade, Prague
ZIDE02	Ivo Žídek	Largo Desolato	Scenic	1990	Theatre on the Balustrade, Prague
ZIDE03	Ivo Žídek	Don Juan	Scenic	1989	Theatre on the Balustrade, Prague
ZIMU01	Sylva Zimula Hanáková	Richard III	Costume	2001	Art Agency Echo, Theatre Globe, Prague

NUMBER	DESIGNER	PRODUCTION	MEDIUM	DATE	VENUE
ZIMU02	Sylva Zimula Hanáková	Richard III	Costume	2001	Art Agency Echo, Theatre Globe, Prague
ZIMU03	Sylva Zimula Hanáková	Richard III	Costume	2001	Art Agency Echo, Theatre Globe, Prague
ZIMU04	Sylva Zimula Hanáková	Richard III	In situ	2001	Art Agency Echo, Theatre Globe, Prague
ZIMU05	Sylva Zimula Hanáková	Richard III	Costume	2001	Art Agency Echo, Theatre Globe, Prague
ZIMU06	Sylva Zimula Hanáková	Richard III	In situ	2001	Art Agency Echo, Theatre Globe, Prague

NOTE: Images in this list are organized numerically; images on the CD list are organized by play.

SELECTED BIBLIOGRAPHY

Albertová, Helena. "An Angel Flying across the Landscape: Otakar Schindler." *Czech Theatre* 9 (May 1995): 20–37.

———. "Even a Disciplined Stage Designer Has His Dreams: Josef Svoboda." *Czech and Slovak Theatre* 4 (December 1992): 52–80.

———, ed. *In Search of Light: The Works of Josef Svoboda*. Prague: Theatre Institute, 1995.

———, ed. *A Mirror of World Theatre II: Prague Quadrennial 1995 and 1999*. Prague: Theatre Institute, 2001.

———, ed. *Otakar Schindler: Stage Designer and Painter*. Prague: Theatre Institute, 1998. A beautiful collection of Schindler's designs and paintings with supporting essays.

———, ed. *The Scenographer's Art: Czech Theatre Stage and Costume Design of the Twentieth Century*. Prague: Theatre Institute, 2003. An exhibition catalog that includes works by Bedřich Feuerstein, Josef Čapek, František Muzika, and many others.

Bezděk, Zdeněk, et al. *DRAK: Twenty-five Years of Existence*. Čelákovice, Czechoslovakia: Tiskarske zavody, 1983. Essays in Czech and pictures from productions designed by Petr Matásek.

Bilková, Marie. "Costume Designs of the Youngest Generation." *Czech Theatre* 14 (June 1998): 45–50. Essays with photos of productions from the last decade of the twentieth century.

———. "Czech Stage Design at the End of the Millenium." *Czech Theatre* 15 (May 1999): 1–8.

———. "Jan Vančura." *Czech and Slovak Theatre* 2 (December 1991): 66–69.

———. "The Puppet through the Eyes of the Visual Artist." *Czech Theatre* 13 (Biannual 1997): 2–20.

———. "The Rough World of Marta Roszkopfová." *Czech Theatre* 11 (May 1996): 43–56.

———. "The World in Images." *Czech Theatre* 15 (May 1999): 9–16.

Brandesky, Joseph, ed. *Metaphor and Irony: Czech Scenic and Costume Design 1920–1999*. Columbus, Ohio: Ohio Arts Council, 2000.

————, ed. *Metaphor and Irony 2: František Tröster and Contemporary Czech Theatre Design*. Prague: Theatre Institute, 2004.

————. "South Bohemian Jewels: Two Faces of Theatre in Český Krumlov." *Slavic and East European Performance* 17, no. 1 (Spring 1997): 19–26. Description of the Baroque Theatre and the Outdoor Theatre with revolving seating at the castle of Český Krumlov. Essay supported by pictures of a production of *Beauty and the Beast* at the outdoor theatre designed by Jaroslav Malina.

Březinová, Pavla. *Year in Review: 2000–2001*. Ostrava, Czech Republic: Národní divadlo Moravskoslezské, 2001. Includes descriptions in Czech of the season and color images of the productions, including those designed by Jaroslav Malina and Helena Anýžová.

————. *Year in Review: 2003–2004*. Ostrava, Czech Republic: Národní divadlo Moravskoslezské, 2004.

Burian, Jarka M. *Leading Creators of Twentieth-Century Czech Theatre*. London: Routledge, 2002.

————. *Modern Czech Theatre: Reflector and Conscience of a Nation*. Iowa City: University of Iowa Press, 2000.

————. *Svoboda: Wagner*. Middletown, CT: Wesleyan University Press, 1983.

Christilles, Dennis. "The Action Design of Jaroslav Malina: Nine Recent Productions." Ph.D. diss., University of Kansas, 1990. Based on Christilles's interviews with Malina and observation of productions in the late eighties.

————, and Delbert Unruh. "The Semiotics of Action Design." *Theatre Topics* 6, no. 2 (September 1996): 121–141.

Confino, Irene Eynat, and Eva Šormová, eds. *Space and the Postmodern Stage*. Prague: Theatre Institute, 2000. Includes an interesting introduction by Jaroslav Malina.

Davis, Tony. *Stage Design*. Switzerland: Rotovision SA, 2001. Jaroslav Malina is listed among the twelve most important designers in the world. The interaction between Malina's designs and his paintings is the subject of an essay supported by color and black-and-white images.

Dubská, Alice. *Czech Puppet Theatre over the Centuries: An Outline of the History of Czech Puppeteering up to 1945*. Prague: International Institute of Puppet Arts, n.d.

————. "From the Hegemony of the Designer to Cooperation in Design." *Czech Theatre* 13 (Biannual 1997): 33–44.

Dvořák, Jan, ed. *Jaroslav Malina*. Prague: Prague Stage, 1999. Four long essays, by Vlasta Gallerová et al., and hundreds of color and black-and-white sketches, renderings, paintings, production photos, and poster designs distinguish this essential record of Malina's creative output.

———, ed. *Josef Krofta: The Tower of Babel*. Hradec Králové, Czech Republic: Prague Stage, 2001. Essays and photos documenting the career one of the guiding forces of the influential puppet company DRAK.

———, ed. *A Plague o' Both Your Houses!!!* Hradec Králové, Czech Republic: Prague Stage, 2001. Essays and photo documentation of an adaptation of *Romeo and Juliet* produced by DRAK and the Japan Foundation.

Erben, Vaclav. *Czech Modern Art 1900–1960*. Prague: National Gallery, 1995.

Hermann, A. H. *A History of the Czechs*. London: Allen Lane, 1975.

Hilmera, Jiří. *František Tröster*. Prague: Theatre Institute, 1989. Essays in Czech supported by black-and-white and color images.

———. *František Tröster: 1904–1968*. Prague: National Museum, 1991. Exhibition catalog.

———. *Theatres of Prague—Short Version*. Prague: Zlatý řez, 1995.

Hořiínek, Zdeněk. "Returns." *Czech and Slovak Theatre* 2 (December 1991): 14–22.

Hošková, Simeona, and Kveta Otcovská, eds. *Jan Švankmajer: Transmutation of the Senses*. Prague: Central Europe Gallery and Publishing House, 2004. Essays, sculptures, paintings, and drawings by the artist best known in the West as a talented filmmaker.

Hrdinová, Radmila. "German Theatre Returns to Bohemia." *Czech Theatre* 21 (June 2005): 25–32. Photos of recent productions, including *Faust*.

Kazda, Jaromír. *A Guide to the History of Czech Theatre*. Prague: Theatre Academy (DAMU), 1994. Digest in English on Czech theatre from its origins until the nineties. Contains a helpful appendix with translations of Czech play titles.

Kolář, Jan. *Twenty-five Years: Studio Ypsilon 1963–1988*. Prague: Tisk Svoboda, 1989. Features many black-and-white photos of productions designed by Miroslav Melena, Jaroslav Malina, and director Jan Schmid.

Král, Karel. "Hanging Man." *Czech Theatre* 14 (June 1998): 41–44.

Kriegeskorte, Werner. *Giuseppe Arcimboldo*. Cologne: Taschen, 1993.

Krofta, Josef, and Zbyněk Vybíral. *DRAK: Thirty Years of Existence*. Červený Kostelec, Czechoslovakia: Severografia, 1988. Includes the production history of DRAK along with essays, black-and-white images, and a brief digest in English.

Kronbauer, Viktor. *The National Theatre 2003–2004*. Prague: Národní divadlo, 2005.

————. "Richard III, through the Lens of Viktor Kronbauer." *Czech Theatre* 18 (August 2002): 5–8. Essay devoted to the production, featuring costumes by Sylva Zimula Hanáková.

Lazorčáková, Tatjana, et al. "The Theatre in Ostrava: A Phenomenon of the Industrial Agglomeration." *Czech Theatre* 20 (June 2004): 3–16.

Lukeš, Milan, and Karel Král. "Marlowe's Dr. Faustus Underground." *Czech Theatre* 18 (August 2002): 14–18. Description of the Alfréd Radok Prize–winning production designed by Petr Matásek.

Machalická, Jana, and Vlasta Gallerová, eds. *Realisticke Divadlo: Divadlo Labyrint, 1985–1996 [Realistic Theatre: Theatre Labyrinth].* Prague: Divaldo Labyrint, 1996. Essays, production photos, and designs by Jaroslav Malina, Marie Franková, Helena Anýžová, and others.

Malíková, Nina. "Puppets in Bohemia." *Czech Theatre* 18 (August 2002): 50–54.

Nešlehová, Mahulena, ed. *Vlastislav Hofman.* Prague: Vlastislav Hofman Society, 2004. A large collection of essays, photos, and designs, covering Hofman's entire life and career.

Nová česka scéna (The New Czech Stage). Prague: Umělecká beseda, 1937. Includes numerous designs (some in color), photos, and essays by, among others, Vlastislav Hofman, Bedřich Feuerstein, František Tröster, and Josef Čapek.

Novotný, J. A. "Puppetmaker: Reflections on Discussions with Jiří Trnka." *Czech Theatre* 13 (Biannual 1997): 56–67.

Orlíková, Jana. *František Tichy.* Prague: Gallery, 2002. Essays and paintings by one of the most important Czech postwar painter-designers.

Patková, Kamila. "How I Lost Myself on Dlouha." *Czech Theatre* 17 (August 2001): 32–36.

Patočková, Jana. "At the End of the 1990s . . . " *Czech Theatre* 14 (June 1998): 2–6.

————. "Faust as a Theatre of the World." *Czech Theatre* 14 (June 1998): 19–26.

Petráněk, Pavel, and Milan Černý. *Daniel Dvořák and Jiří Nekvasil and Their Theatre.* Prague: Národní divadlo, 2004. Color photographs of productions along with essays, designs, and black-and-white process sketches.

Pomajzlová, Alena. *Josef Čapek: The Humblest Art.* Prague: Municipal House, 2003. Graphics, paintings, theatre designs, and essays covering the career of Karel Čapek's brother and artistic collaborator.

Prchalová, Radka. *Collage of Eight: National Section of the Czech Exposition, Prague Quadrennial 1999.* Prague: Theatre Institute, 1999. Biographies and images of the Czech artists who were awarded the Golden Triga at the 1999 Prague Quadrennial.

Ptáčková, Věra. *Česka scénografie XX. stoleti* [*Czech Scenography of the Twentieth Century*]. Prague: Odeon, 1982. Beginning with the design by František Muzika on the cover, this book is a testament to the variety and talent of twentieth-century Czech theatre designers. Among the treasures to be found in this edition are designs by Vlastislav Hofman, Antonín Heythum, Bedřich Feuerstein, Josef Wenig, František Zelenka, Josef Čapek, Jan Sládek, Miroslav Kouřil, Libor Fára, František Tröster, Jaroslav Malina, and Josef Svoboda, to name but a few.

———. "Jan Dušek." *Czech Theatre* 15 (May 1999): 17–20. Essay and designs by the current head of the scenography section at DAMU.

———. *A Mirror of World Theatre: The Prague Quadrennial 1967–1991*. Prague: Theatre Institute, 1995.

———. "The Roots and Distinctions of Modern Czech Stage Design." *Czech and Slovak Theatre* 5 (July 1993): 54–72.

———. "Space Changes." *Czech Theatre* 9 (May 1995): 2–18.

Reslová, Marie. "The Rhythmic Exorcisms of J.A.P. [Jan Antonín Pitínský]." *Czech Theatre* 14 (June 1998): 32–38.

———. "Silence Is Sexy." *Czech Theatre* 20 (June 2004): 29–41.

———. "Zábradlí [Theatre on the Balustrade] after Lébl." *Czech Theatre* 21 (June 2005): 11–20. Includes production photos of designs by Kateřina Štefková shown in Metaphor and Irony 2.

Rutte, Miroslav, and Josef Kodiček, eds. *Nové české divadlo 1918–1926* [*The New Czech Theatre*]. Prague: Aventinum, 1927. Essays in Czech with many illustrations by Vlastislav Hofman (including a costume design) and František Muzika and a color set piece designed by Josef Čapek.

———. *Nové české divadlo 1927*. Prague: Aventinum, 1928. Essays in Czech by Hofman and others, sketches by Hofman and Muzika, and photos of costumes designed by Hofman.

———. *Nové české divadlo 1928–30*. Prague: Aventinum, 1931. Essays in Czech by Hofman and others; production photos.

———. *Nové české divadlo 1930–32*. Prague: Aventinum, 1933. Essays, photos, and designs.

Scherhaufer, Peter. *Inscenování v nepravidelném prostoru*. Ostrava: Krajské kulturní středisko, 1989.

Šimáčková, Sylva, and Josef Zubák, eds. *Salon Scenografie 95*. Prague: Asociace scénografu, 1995. With a Czech introduction by Marie Bilková and preface by Jaroslav Malina, this edition includes photos, sketches, and renderings by sixty-eight designers.

Sloupová, Jitka. "The Diabolical Angel of the Czech Theatre." *Czech Theatre* 20 (June 2004): 17–26.

———. "A Farewell to the Nineties." *Czech Theatre* 14 (April 2000): 6–19.

———. "Is This Drawn from Life?" *Czech Theatre* 14 (June 1998): 27–31.

———. "Theatre without Respite." *Czech Theatre* 17 (August 2001): 25–31.

Tetiva, Vlastimil. *František Muzika [and] Zdeněk Sklenář: Kontakty, Kontrasty, Konfrontace [Contacts, Contrasts, Confrontations]*. České Budějovice, Czech Republic: Alšova Jihočeská Galerie v Hluboké nad Vltavou [Alšova South Bohemian Gallery at Hluboka on the Vltava], 2004. Paintings by two artists who designed for Czech theatres.

Unruh, Delbert. "Action Design." *Theatre Design and Technology* 23 (Spring 1987): 6–13.

———. "Practical Problems of Space." *Theatre Design and Technology* 26 (Summer 1990): 33–40.

———. "Philosophical Problems of Space." *Theatre Design and Technology* 26 (Fall 1990): 25–32.

———. "The Problem of Acting Style." *Theatre Design and Technology* 27 (Summer 1991): 21–29.

———. "The Problem of Costumes." *Theatre Design and Technology* 27 (Winter 1991): 27–34.

———. *Towards a New Theatre: The Lectures of Robert Edmond Jones*. New York: Limelight Editions, 1992.

———. *USITT Presents the Designs of Ming Cho Lee*. Louisville, KY: UITT and Broadway Press, 2006.

Uršič, Giorgio Ursini, ed. *Josef Svoboda: Scenographer*. Florence: Union of the Theatres of Europe, 1999. The best collection currently available on Svoboda's design legacy, includes excerpts from Svoboda's explanation of his process as well as his early renderings and numerous production photos.

Vitochová, Marie, et al. *Prague and Art Nouveau*. Prague: V RÁJI Publishing House, 1995. Photos of the Vinohrady Theatre and other art nouveau monuments in Prague.

Vlček, Tomáš, ed. *The Museum of Czech Cubism*. Prague: National Gallery, 2004. Essays and items in the collection. Particularly interesting are Vlastislav Hofman's cubist chairs and other examples of applied art.

Vlnas, Vít, ed. *Mannerist and Baroque Art in Bohemia*. Prague: National Gallery, 2005.

Walters, E. Garrison. *The Other Europe: Eastern Europe to 1945*. New York: Dorset Press, 1990.

Zdeňková, Marie. *Czech Made: Contemporary Czech Stage Design.* Prague: Theatre Institute, 2003. Artist biographies and excerpts of reviews are combined with photos and black-and-white and color renderings.

———. "Czech Stage Design Reflected in the Prague Quadrennial." *Czech Theatre* 19 (May 2003): 5–16.

———. "Theatre of Pictures: Interview with David Marek, Curator of the Czech Exposition at PQ 2003." *Czech Theatre* 19 (May 2003): 17–22.

STUDIES IN THEATRE HISTORY & CULTURE